JAPAN AND THE WIDER WORLD

From the Mid-nineteenth Century to the Present

Akira Iriye

LONGMAN
London and New York

Addison Wesley Longman Limited
Edinburgh Gate
Harlow
Essex CM20 2JE
United Kingdom
and Associated Companies throughout the world

Published in the United States of America
by Addison Wesley Longman Inc., New York
© Chuokoron-Sha, Inc. 1997

First published 1997

ISBN 0 582 21054 2 CSD
ISBN 0 582 21053 4 PPR

British Library Cataloguing-in-Publication Data

A catalogue record for this book is available from the British Library

Library of Congress Cataloging-in-Publication Data

Iriye, Akira.
    Japan and the wider world: from the mid-nineteenth century to the
present / Akira Iriye.
        p. cm.
Includes bibliographical references and index.
ISBN 0-582-21054-2. – ISBN 0-582-21053-4 (pbk.)
1. Japan–Foreign relations–1868– I. Title.
DS881.96.I75 1997
327.52–dc21   96-39690
                                                                                        CIP

Set by 7R
Produced by Longman Singapore Publishers (Pte) Ltd.
Printed in Singapore

JAPAN AND THE WIDER WORLD

CONTENTS

FOREWORD

This book is based on two little volumes I have published in Japan: *Nihon no gaikō* (Japanese diplomacy, 1965) and *Shin Nihon no gaikō* (Japanese diplomacy since the war, 1991). Both volumes aim at examining the intellectual foundations (or lack thereof) of Japanese foreign affairs since the 'opening' of the country in the mid-nineteenth century. Rather than being a chronological survey of diplomatic events, they offer my interpretation of the ways in which Japanese policy-makers and their critics ('public opinion') have viewed their country's position and role in the world. The basic assumption here is that the foreign affairs of any country are built on certain ideas and images about a number of communities: national, regional, global, as well as subnational. How a country defines itself, consisting as it does of numerous groups and localities; how national leaders view regional and global 'realities'; and what meanings they, and various opinion-asserting bodies, give to their country's place in the history and geography of the world – these questions provide a point of departure, as well as of continuity, as we study international relations. In this book the reader will note that particular emphasis is given to such themes as Japanese images of the Western powers, cooperation and/or competition with the West, East–West relations, and pan-Asianism. This is because these themes were almost always at the basis of policy decisions by Japanese officials, and of assertions by their opponents. 'Japan and the wider world', then, does not just describe the contents of the book; it provides the key framework, the mental universe, in which the Japanese people and their leaders have sought to understand their place and their role in the international community.

The original volumes have been rather well received in Japan, and many people have suggested that I have them translated into English. Instead of presenting a verbatim translation, however, I have decided to make a few changes and add (or delete) a word or a sentence here and there so that the two separate books will smoothly combine into one. Because more than a quarter century elapsed between the writings of the two books, some of my interpretations and conceptual schemes inevitably changed in the meantime, but my interest in viewing international affairs as phenomena in intellectual as well as diplomatic history remains.

I am grateful to the staff of Addison Wesley Longman, for first proposing the project and for having carefully examined the draft translation, and to my original publisher, Chûôkôron, for granting me permission to undertake an English translation. I am only sorry that it has taken rather long, more than three years since the project was first conceived, to complete the translation.

September 1996   A.I.

Chapter 1

THE ORIGINS OF MODERN
JAPANESE DIPLOMACY

The history of modern Japanese foreign policy begins with
the Meiji Restoration of 1868 which put an end to the reign
of the Tokugawa shogunate (since the early seventeenth
century) and established a new government under the
emperor whose palace was moved to Tokyo, the new capital.
By then a number of treaties had been signed with Western
powers to regulate trade and other matters, and the new
Meiji government started out by acknowledging the validity
of these treaties. The powers, on their part, extended
diplomatic recognition to Tokyo. But, even though
Tokugawa officials had dealt with foreign affairs, the Meiji
leaders had to learn much about the conduct of diplomacy,
about international affairs in general, and, most fundamentally, about the West, its people and its culture.

A good example of this learning experience may be read
in Iwakura Tomomi's exhortation to his countrymen in
1869: 'all human beings have horizontal eyes and vertical
noses. Even if their hair is red and eyes blue, they are all
human, endowed with their ideas of loyalty, filial piety, and
marital affection. We should not despise them as barbarians
but treat them as courteously as we would friends.' Iwakura,
a court noble, was one of the young leaders of the Meiji
government who, in 1871–73, led an embassy to the United
States and Europe, the first official mission dispatched by
the Meiji state. He, like his colleagues, was acutely aware of
the need to appeal to his countrymen to overcome their
anti-foreign prejudices, products of their over two hundred
years' isolation from the rest of the world (except for China
and the Netherlands, with which limited trade had been

carried on even before the 1850s). Iwakura and other leaders knew that not only Japan's existence as an independent nation but also the very survival of the Meiji regime would be jeopardized if anti-foreign fanatics created incidents – as they had done during the decades preceding the Restoration – and brought about foreign intervention; that, too, had happened earlier in Japan and, as they were well aware, in China.

It is important to note that even at this early stage, Meiji leaders spoke of the need 'to protect the independence of the imperial nation [kôkoku]' as the fundamental objective of their foreign policy. But how could such an objective be attained? Not, any longer, by maintaining a self-righteous isolation from world affairs or indulging in anti-foreign violence but by 'following the motions of the universe'. Diplomatic intercourse was seen as an inevitable 'motion' governing relations among nations, and Japan could not be excepted if it were to survive. But the Japanese knew that the 'universe' in this context essentially meant the Western powers. Whereas before the 1850s China had provided the mental universe in which affairs of state could be discussed, there was a quick shift of focus from China to the West. Having decided that international relations were, for all intents and purposes, those defined by the nations of Europe and North America, Tokyo's officials from early on tried to find out what lay behind the rise and growth of these countries' power and influence in the world.

What constituted a nation's power? How could it be augmented? It so happened that these questions, which European statesmen and scholars had been debating since the seventeenth century, were giving rise to some fresh perspectives and novel answers in the West during the 1870s, just when the Japanese were becoming obsessed with the issue of national independence. It may be said that this fortuitous circumstance facilitated Japan's quest for the secrets of the West's power. Japanese leaders like Iwakura and Ōkubo Toshimichi, perhaps the most powerful politician in the early Meiji period till he was assassinated in 1878, carefully observed Western nations during their world tour of 1871–73 and became convinced that ultimately the power of the Western nations derived from their modern political and economic systems: the coalescing of people's energies, the enhancing of their national consciousness through education, and the development of industry. Without such changes, mere military strengthening would not build national power. As they travelled to Europe and America, Iwakura, Ōkubo, and many others learned that the masses paid attenton to national political affairs, that governments took pains to promote the welfare of the people. Government and people together then cooperated to enhance the power of the respective nations. Of course, the situation varied from country to country, and many other features distinguished Western nations, but the Meiji leaders were determined that political and economic reforms must take precedence over all others.

Such perceptions produced specific programmes for Japan's transformation. Politically, a constitutional monarchy patterned after the British and German examples was established, along with centralized systems of bureaucracy and education. These reforms could be undertaken without incurring too many diplomatic complications, but economic reforms were a different story. Without tariff autonomy, it was extremely difficult to develop indigenous industry; imported goods paid a minimum of customs duties, while exports had to be shipped abroad through the intermediary of foreign merchants residing in the open ports, where they enjoyed extraterritorial privileges. As Baba Tatsui, a political thinker who studied in Britain during the 1870s, wrote in 1876, so long as Western merchants enjoyed the unjust and improper privileges of extraterritoriality, Japan's commerce would only be destined to weaken and national wealth would be exhausted. Treaty revision was absolutely imperative if Japan were to strengthen its economic bases, not to mention upholding its national dignity. The government, sharing such views, was determined from early on to bring about the modification and ultimate abolition of the unequal treaties. 'Achieving equality with other nations', in the words of Sanjō Sanetomi, like Iwakura a court nobleman who occupied high posts in the early Meiji government, was thus considered an essential part of the programme for national strengthening.

At the back of such determination was a widely shared image of the West as a group of modernized nations. If Japan were to survive as an independent nation, it must be like them, politically and economically. Of course, this implied optimism that Japanese could undertake what the Westerners had accomplished. Modernization and Westernization were interchangeable. This was what Fukuzawa Yukichi, perhaps the most influential writer at that time, meant by his call for 'leaving Asia'; so long as Japan remained entrapped in traditional Asian ways, it could never achieve full independence. Japan could grow only if it 'marched alongside the civilized nations of the world', as he said. It should be noted that the West was not considered intrinsically either good or evil but was viewed pragmatically, as an object of emulation. The value lay not so much in the West as in the act of emulating the West. Westernization would not make Japan any more moral than it was, nor would it be used to oppose the West for some ulterior purposes. Modern transformation was not a moralistic proposition but rather an amoral (not necessarily immoral) prescription for national survival. Meiji Japanese diplomacy, therefore, may be said to have been characterized by realism and pragmatism, implying an absence of moralistic considerations.

That could best be seen in national security policy. To defend the homeland, it would of course be necessary to strengthen national defences, but what should be the policy towards the neighbouring countries? How much military force was necessary for possible use there? Here again, Japanese leaders were influenced by their perception of the West, that the Western powers appeared to be rapidly extending power to Southeast Asia, China, and Korea. Should they fall under the control of Western powers, Japan's security would be compromised. Japan must, therefore, be prepared to prevent such penetration either by placing some of the areas under its own control or by other means. The incorporation of Okinawa into Japanese jurisdiction (1879) and the 'exchange' of South Sakhalin for the Kurile islands through a treaty with Russia (1875) were examples of such thinking. Likewise, it was considered imperative to prevent Korea and its environs (the Strait of Tsushima, the Yellow Sea) from falling under great-power control. The policy of seeking Korean 'independence' did not necessarily mean Japan must expand into the peninsula, but that it should not be allowed to become another power's protectorate or colony.

All these policies required military strengthening, and systematic efforts in that direction began in the 1880s. As Sanjō noted in 1882, after the Meiji restoration it had been necessary to 'rest the people and build up basic resources', but it had become 'unfortunately unavoidable, given world conditions, to strengthen our army and navy'. In the 1870s a system of conscription was instituted to produce manpower for regular forces, a General Staff was organized to serve the emperor as commander-in-chief, and a naval construction plan was drafted. And in the following decade, in order to fund these projects, while at the same time controlling inflation that had accompanied the political turmoil and economic change after 1868, a fiscal retrenchment policy was carried out under the leadership of Matsukata Masayoshi, finance minister for many years after 1881; state-owned factories were sold to private entrepreneurs, the use of inconvertible paper currencies was controlled, a central bank (the Bank of Japan) was established to issue convertible notes, and indirect taxes were increased. The Matsukata policy ultimately aimed at increasing exports and reducing imports, but such a policy could not be carried out until Japan regained tariff autonomy. So Tokyo redoubled its efforts to achieve this objective as well. In other words, there was cohesiveness and unity to Japanese political and diplomatic objectives, at least until around 1890. That is, Japanese diplomacy was interchangeable with efforts at modernization. When Inoue Kaoru, one of the principal negotiators for treaty revision during the 1870s and the 1880s, asserted that 'we must make our nation and people into a European nation and European people', he was expressing the widely accepted view that national independence, treaty revision, and modern transformation were all aspects of the same agenda, that of emulating the powerful and advanced Western nations. Although Meiji leaders often engaged in acrimonious debate, for instance concerning the best means of abolishing extraterritoriality, they shared essentially this same perspective on Japan's domestic and foreign affairs.

It is interesting to note that, in the 1870s and 1880s, precisely at the moment that Meiji leaders were developing basic principles of Japanese diplomacy, Europeans and Americans, too, were defining new conceptions of national and international affairs. It may be more correct to say that these conceptions were not so much new as reformulations of the seventeenth- and eighteenth-century notions of mercantilism. In the nineteenth century, anti- mercantilist perspectives, for instance stressing free trade, *laissez-faire*, and the primacy of economics in domestic and world politics, had been quite influential. But by the 1870s and 1880s, they had begun to be superseded by a renewed emphasis on the role of the state in economic affairs as well as broadened conceptions of national interest and security. Earlier, national interest had been seen in terms of economic development under conditions of free trade, but now voices began advocating an expanded definition. For example, in Germany Alfred G. Schlieffen stressed the importance of maintaining stable domestic order as a requirement for national defence; in France L. H. G. Lyautey asserted that military officers must be sensitive to social issues; in Britain Joseph Chamberlain gave colonialism an emotional justification as a necessary link to the defence of the motherland; and in Russia Sergei Witte advocated the economic penetration of neighbouring lands through state initiative and support. These men believed that 'rational' economic development pursued under *laissez-faire* conditions did not necessarily protect national interests and were calling for the formation of a new national policy that viewed military and economic affairs as means for ensuring the nation's security and other interests. Economic forces, which had been assumed to be 'rational' and 'inter-nationalized', transcending 'artificial' entities such as nation-states, were now to be seen as means for the implementation of state policies.

How such a shift took place has long been debated, but clearly technological innovations were a crucial factor. Advances in manufacturing and communications technology were producing more goods for markets, shortening distances between nations, obliterating local autonomies, enabling nations to exercise greater control over different colonies, awakening people's awareness of the world through newspapers and travels, and arousing their interest in public affairs so that their ideas, emotions, and prejudices would have to be taken seriously by governments. These developments heightened the sense that traditional economic theories, diplomatic concepts, or political ideologies were no longer sufficient and that efforts would have to be made to construct a new world view.

The reformulation of national security was a good example. Technological changes were already causing a redefinition of the concept of national defence. Schlieffen, for instance, early noted the strategic roles to be played by railways and telegrams, while Alfred Thayer Mahan in the United States advocated a new naval policy to correspond to developments in shipbuilding technology. Beyond such purely military matters, statesmen and intellectuals in the West became increasingly interested in broadening the definition of security, for instance discussing the relationship between domestic social order and national defence. The adoption of conscription and protective tariffs in most Western nations towards the end of the nineteenth century fitted into such a trend, as did the renewed expansion into Asia and Africa after the 1880s. In the so-called 'age of Bismarck', the European powers managed to maintain a degree of equilibrium among themselves through an intricate system of ententes so that the development of new technology led to inter-power conflicts primarily in countries outside Europe. Overseas colonies' economic importance had been emphasized since the sixteenth century, but now their political and military significance was stressed.

These territories, in other words, came to be seen as part of world geopolitical equations, with bases in the colonies, for example, contributing to the growth of the imperialists' naval power. Intellectually, all these views reflected an effort to incorporate the technological developments and, in particular, earth's shrinking distances into a redefinition of national interest. Events in distant parts of the globe were seen to be of immediate relevance to national power and security. Before the 1890s, however, the powers' primary concern was with Africa, South and Southeast Asia, and the Pacific Ocean, rather than East Asia. They had not yet extended their territorial control and struggles for power to that corner of the world. As if to take advantage of this relative indifference, the Ch'ing empire in China undertook a 'self-strengthening' movement, involving the strengthening of the navy and the encouragement of industrialization through the system of 'official supervision and merchant management'.

This was the international environment in which Japan made its appearance in the world scene under the Meiji government. There was thus a congruence between Japan's policies, pursuing treaty revision, military strengthening, and other programmes for modernization, and the realities of world conditions. The Japanese were determined not to be left behind in the waves of technological change and to incorporate the advanced nations' industrial techniques, strategic concepts, and ideologies of national interest. Even with regard to treaty revision, the key to the nation's ability to conduct modern diplomacy, it was a fortuitous circumstance that the Western powers were not yet engaged in a fierce struggle for power in East Asia. The realities as perceived by Japanese leaders and their definition of national priorities and defence strategies were closely matched, it may be said, because there was no gap between the 'realities' and the 'perceived realities'. In thus perceiving the 'realities', Japanese leaders avoided abstract theorizing or moralizing, preferring instead to persist in a pragmatic, even a non-ideological approach to foreign affairs.

This last point, namely that abstract thinking and theory were lacking in early Meiji diplomacy, was actually to become a major characteristic of the subsequent history as well. Those in power eschewed moralism and emotionalism and sought to focus on specific problem-solving. Such a stance gave rise to criticism on the part of those outside the seat of power. They advocated an expedition to Korea right after the Meiji Restoration, condemned the slow-going treaty revision negotiations as 'humiliating' to the nation, denounced programmes for Westernization, and advocated active policies to encourage reforms in Korea and China. They were not satisfied with the government's pragmatism and called for a more colourful diplomacy, a more moralistic approach to world problems, or a more emotional formulation of national policies. These attacks themselves reveal that Meiji diplomacy was indeed colourless and devoid of abstract ideology.

It may be said that the government's approach was almost always 'realistic', whereas the critics were seeking a more 'idealistic' foreign policy. For instance, the Meiji state's realism accepted the 'realities' of world politics which were, as they said, creating a situation where 'the strong ate the meat of the weak'. In such a situation, if Japan were to survive, it had no choice but to try to become like one of the strong. Some of the opponents, on their part, argued that there was no point in merely emulating the Western powers and that Japan should try to coalesce the rest of Asia in opposition to them.

The opponents included former samurai (feudal warriors) now dispossessed of their privileges, as well as politicians, journalists, and scholars dissatisfied with the pace or direction of the Meiji state's modernization pro- grammes. They did not quite amount to public opinion in the Western sense; even after the constitution was promulgated in 1889, the right to vote was limited to a fraction of the male population, and numerous political parties came and went without developing anything resembling a multi-party parliamentary system. Still, an open- ended discussion of public affairs was something new in the country, and the emergence, in the early Meiji period, of divergent views on international affairs is of considerable interest, for they anticipated some of the key themes in the history of modern Japanese foreign relations.

One important theme was what may be characterized as an Asianist orientation, as against the government's preoccupation with the West. Whether they followed the lead of Gen'yōsha (the Wide Ocean Society) advocating that Japan should make itself the leader in Asia, or of Nakae Chōmin, Ono Azusa, and other 'people's rights' advocates insisting that the nation should help other Asian countries achieve freedom and independence, a number of publicists were advocating a pan-Asianist agenda which stressed the solidarity of all Asian countries and was thus diametrically opposed to the government's policy of Westernization. The Asianists argued that Japan's mission lay in its Asian identity. A moralistic or an emotional formulation of foreign policy would result from such a perspective, in contrast to the government's steady refusal to listen to pan-Asianist rhetoric in order to concentrate on solving treaty, territorial, and other immediate issues. The more it succeeded in achieving results in this regard, the louder became the voices of the

Asianists, some undoubtedly pursuing a vision of Asian freedom.

The opposition between realism and idealism characterizes many countries' foreign policies, but in Japan's case it may be said that the opposition took the form of the state's realism and the public's idealism, although the bulk of the 'public' may have stood outside such controversy. Japan did not yet have a fully developed civil society; as Fukuzawa said: 'We have a state but no nation in Japan.' The fact remains that while the non-ideological, non-emotional pragmatism of the government paid off in many respects, the very successes served to widen the gap between it and its opponents.

Chapter 2

THE EMERGENCE OF JAPAN AS A GREAT POWER

In an 1890 memorandum on Japanese foreign and military affairs, Prime Minister Yamagata Aritomo, a principal architect of the country's military modernization, pointed out that 'the way to the nation's independence and security' lay in defining and defending its 'line of sovereignty' and 'line of interest'. The former included the Japan homeland which, of course, was the primary objective of national defence, but in order to ensure this objective, the nation must be prepared to defend the areas defined by the line of interest, namely neighbouring areas that 'have an intimate relationship to the homeland's security'. At that moment, Yamagata wrote, no foreign power appeared likely to threaten the security of Japan proper, but the nation could never rest assured unless it established control over the line of interest. If, within that line, 'another power should act in such a way as to bring disadvantages to us, we must be willing to eject such a power resolutely, even by using force if necessary'.

As can be seen here, the definition of the line of interest was rather vague. Yamagata meant areas that were deemed relevant to the security of the homeland, but the security of the homeland was said to depend on securing control over these areas. This was circular reasoning, but Meiji leaders had indulged in such thinking from early on, as revealed in their ambiguous attitude towards Korea. By 1890, however, these ideas took on an air of specific urgency, convincing Yamagata and others that the time had come to act with determination to ensure Korean 'independence', in other words, to include the peninsula within Japan's line of

11

interest. They were particularly mindful of Russian policy, recognizing that the construction of the Siberian Railway was about to begin and that, when it was completed, not only would Korean independence be threatened but Japan's line of sovereignty, including the Tsushima islands, 'would be in danger as if a dagger were being held above them'. In order to cope with the situation, not only should the nation strengthen its army and navy, but it should coordinate action with Britain, Germany, and other powers interested in Korean autonomy so as to develop 'an association of nations sharing common interests in East Asia'. But, Yamagata warned, to complete such steps might require more than twenty years; the Japanese, therefore, must persevere ('lying among firewood and licking one's own liver') till the nation's survival was finally ensured.

The memorandum gives a good indication of how Japan's leaders were viewing external affairs, now that domestic affairs had become more or less stabilized with the promulgation of the constitution (1889) and the convening of the Diet (1890). In outline, there was little in Yamagata's ideas that had not existed earlier, but his insistence on bringing Korea within Japan's line of interest was to be diligently followed by Japanese leaders until the outbreak of the Russo-Japanese war in 1904. Although he had predicted that it would take more than twenty years to achieve this end, the nation managed by 1905 not only to establish control over Korea but to incorporate Taiwan into its territory and extend its influence over Fukien province in China, opposite Taiwan, thus emerging as a fully-fledged imperialist power.

How did Japan, seeking desperately to liberate itself from the restrictions imposed by the Western powers and to modernize itself, launch an imperialistic career? Was there no alternative? What was to be Japan's role in the imperialistic world system? Much would of course depend on what is understood by the term 'imperialism'. Even among Marxist scholars it has been subject to much controversy, and there is too easy (and dangerous) a tendency to read concerns and judgements over contemporary issues back into the term. Some argue that Japanese imperialism was a historical inevitability, others that it was morally reprehensible, while still others assert

12

that it was not as pernicious as Western imperialism, even that it was not imperialistic at all. In discussing this and other phenomena, we should try as much as possible to be free from dogmatism, emotionalism, and contemporary political preoccupations and to understand past phenomena in their context. Understanding the past, of course, is not the same thing as morally defending or condemning it.

One way of understanding Japan's imperialistic diplomacy is to examine the images of international affairs held by the nation's leaders. For instance, the above-cited memorandum by Yamagata noted that not only Russia's Siberian Railway but also the Canadian railways being built by Britain indicated how easy it had become, due to improvements in transportation technology, to traverse the earth, enabling the Western powers to advance into Asia much more expeditiously than earlier. 'The days when there is peace in the West', Yamagata concluded, 'are therefore the time for them to contemplate long-term strategies for the East.' As a result, 'the heritages and resources of the East are like so many pieces of meat about to be devoured by tigers'. Such an image of the Western powers had existed before, but now it had assumed greater specificity and reality because of the technological developments, giving rise to the fear that Western power rivalries would spill over into Asia, enveloping it in further turmoil.

There was also a second theme that became noticeable in the 1890s, namely the idea that the Western powers were not merely scheming to obtain more territory in Asia but also intent upon expanding their trade and economic interests in the region as part of their power rivalries. The Meiji leaders had, as noted earlier, always been aware that economic resources were the basis of a nation's power, but now they began talking of a 'peacetime war', to use an expression made popular by Itō Hirobumi, Yamagata's civilian counterpart and political rival during these decades. The term referred to the powers' continuing struggle to expand trade and investment opportunities abroad so as to further augment their power. There was the fear that Asia might become the arena for such 'peacetime warfare', in addition to more openly imperialistic schemes.

To cope with such a situation, Yamagata, Itō, and other

13

leaders saw no alternative to following the example of the Western powers and doing likewise. As Kurino Shin'ichirō, minister to France, stated to Foreign Minister Ōkuma Shigenobu in 1897, the powers' attention was shifting to Asia, in particular China, making it likely that they would soon interfere in China's internal affairs through a 'coalition of the European powers'. Under the circumstances, Kurino wrote, Japan's best strategy lay in joining this 'European coalition' in order to 'obtain substantial rights and interests'. But the powers would admit Japan into their coalition only if the nation could justify its position as one of the great powers, and in order to do so Japan should 'either invest its capital in railways, industry, etc. in China or extend loans to that country'. Such views constituted the ideological basis of Japanese foreign policy at the turn of the century. Japan's security was deemed to lie in the establishment of a superior position over the neighbouring areas, or else in preventing a third power from establishing such control. Furthermore, it seemed important to create Japan's spheres of influence so as to become one of the powers playing the game of power politics in the world arena. In pursuing such a policy, the nation should not aim at opposing the Western imperialist powers but at co-operating with as many of them as possible so that they would recognize Japan's position in Asia. At bottom was a view of the world as being divided into the great powers on one hand and their colonies or semi-colonies on the other. Japan's security and position clearly seemed to lie in identifying with the great powers.

There was an element of realism in such thinking. From the 1880s the powers did become interested in Asia, as seen in such developments as the British–Russian rivalry in the Korean peninsula and Central Asia, the British–French clash in South China and Southeast Asia, German expansion into China, and the US annexation of Hawaii and the Philippines. Asia and the Pacific were fast becoming arenas for imperialist politics. It was assumed that the powers' positions in the region would be immediately reflected in their status in Europe, and that the bases and markets they obtained in Asia would contribute to the wealth and power of the mother countries. At the same time, none of them wished to see too abrupt a change in the balance of power and so sought to prevent a power from becoming too predominant here as well as elsewhere. The result was that while imperialistic rivalries were intense, inter-power relations in Asia, Africa, and the Middle East could also define a status quo, no matter how temporary.

Japan tried to fit itself into the prevailing system of international relations by expanding into Korea and Taiwan without disrupting the status quo too precipitously. The success of such an effort would, of course, depend on the attitude of the powers, and here the record was mixed, as can be seen in Japanese diplomacy during the Chinese war. The war (1894–95) involved the two countries' conflicting policies in Korea, but Japan was paying close attention to the responses of the powers so as to prevent their joint intervention. In this the Japanese were successful, but when they insisted on the cession of Liaotung peninsula they met with strong opposition on the part of Germany, France, and Russia. The triple intervention was clearly a failure of Japanese diplomacy and indicated that from the powers' point of view Japan had significantly upset the regional status quo. It was not surprising, then, that Japanese diplomacy after the intervention was extremely cautious, focusing on the typically imperialistic policy of steadily building its spheres of influence while maintaining political understandings with the powers. A good example was Japan's participation in the 1901 international expedition to suppress anti-foreign mobs in China, known as the Boxers. As they besieged the legation quarters in Peking, severing the connection between the capital and the port city of Tientsin, six European powers, the United States, and Japan sent an expedition to fight the Boxers and liberate the entrapped foreigners. Japan's participation in the effort demonstrated its emergence as a great power whose position in China would have to be reckoned with by other great powers.

But Japan's primary concern still lay with the Korean peninsula. Intent upon bringing it under its sphere of influence, it worked hard to obtain other powers' acknowledgement of this special position. The alliance with Britain, signed in 1902, and the negotiations with Russia that started in 1903 were means for this end. These negotiations were based on the assumption that in the end

15

Russia, like other powers, would accept Japanese control over Korea. As such optimism proved premature – some of the contradictory information was fabricated by the army – Tokyo ultimately judged that Russia was not likely to accept Korea's falling under Japanese domination, concluding that war with Russia could not be avoided. But whether achieved through diplomacy or through war, the establishment of Japan's special position in Korea implied its military and economic presence there, which would inevitably threaten Russia's position in south Manchuria and the Maritime province. So, in either event, Japanese–Russian conflict was in the picture throughout these years. In any event, on 21 April 1903, four of Japan's foremost leaders, former Prime Ministers Yamagata and Itō, Prime Minister Katsura Tarō, and Foreign Minister Komura Jutarō, met in Kyoto's Murin-an, an inn, and decided that the nation should 'never give up Korea no matter what difficulties are encountered'. This was tantamount to a decision for war.

Besides Korea, Japan was also trying to emulate the imperialist powers by expanding into Taiwan and, with the island as a foothold, into mainland China, in particular Fukien province. This was the time when it seemed as if the powers were about to partition China. Japan, it was believed, could not be left behind. But because economically Japan was far behind the Western powers, the best strategy seemed to lie in making use of Taiwan as the jumping-off place to try to turn Fukien and its environs into Japanese spheres of influence. This was referred to as a 'southern policy' and underscored the felt necessity to expand into China proper in order to promote national interests. As a cabinet decision declared at the end of 1903: 'The basic objectives of our policy for the continent of Asia are, in the north, to perfect our defence system through maintaining Korean independence [sic] and, in the south, to bring south China into our sphere of influence from our base in Fukien.'

Such a policy presupposed a certain image of China. The above-quoted Kurino memorandum indicated that already in the wake of the Chinese–Japanese war, there was concern that China might become dominated or divided by the great powers. But after the Boxer uprising, there also grew the view that the Ch'ing dynasty might disintegrate because of internal causes. Foreign Minister Komura, for instance, noted in 1904 that China 'cannot be expected to maintain its independence or territorial integrity through its own resources; therefore, it seems possible that it will ultimately become fragmented'. This was a typical image of China which Japanese officials entertained at that time. Combined with their image of the powerful West, such a view of China inevitably produced the fear that once that country began to disintegrate, the powers would only be too ready to enter into the scene and expand their respective spheres of influence.

To cope with such an eventuality, the Japanese began making plans for their own expansion into China even while they professed their support for the principles of its administrative and territorial integrity. As Komura said, 'the great problem' of how to dispose of China was certain to arise in the near future, and Japan must 'establish a basis for partaking in such disposition from a position of strength'. But how could Japan, a late-comer to the scene and far inferior economically to the Western powers, compete with them in entrenching its influence in China? No ordinary means would do, it was widely believed, and the nation must be prepared to make use of special methods and strategies. As the Ministry of Agriculture and Commerce pointed out in 1902, 'since we are no match for the Western nations in capital, the only way we can compete with them is through knowledge and technology'. It would be important, for instance, to establish networks for gathering information throughout China, and to work closely with the Chinese in building railways.

There was a danger, however, that openly seeking a special relationship with China, or merely giving such an impression, might arouse the suspicion of the Western nations and incur their pre-emptive intervention. Japanese leaders were extremely sensitive about the 'yellow perilist' fears in the West and worried that any talk of Japan's special position in Asia or close ties with China might provoke the West's suspicion – what they termed 'yellow-phobia' – and bring about its collective reprisal, such as the tripartite intervention of 1895. The alliance with Britain was in part intended to allay such fears. That, and other policies at this time, in a way reflected the inferiority complex of a country lacking in military and economic power comparable to that of the West and the determination to safeguard the nation's security and interests by playing the game of imperialism, not through any pan-Asianist scheme.

Thus Japanese diplomacy after 1890 sought to turn the nation into a great power and to establish control over neighbouring territory, without alienating the West. The policy succeeded in the sense that the Western powers did not obstruct Japanese expansion into Taiwan or Fukien province. While Russia stood in the way of Japanese designs in Korea, in the end Japan managed to isolate that power. The great powers' diplomacy of imperialism, in other words, on the whole accommodated Japanese ambitions.

Underneath such surface successes, however, several serious problems were already becoming apparent. One was the growth of domestic opposition to official policy. Towards China, in particular, some opinion leaders were critical of the policy of cautious expansion in the framework of cooperation with the Western powers. A good example of non-governmental opinion was Nakae Chōmin's *San suijin keirin mondō* (Three drunkards' debate on public affairs), published in 1887. The three drunkards represented, first, the official 'realist' position, stressing the need for caution and for cooperation with the West; second, the Asianist view that ridiculed the government's deference to the West and insisted, instead, on unilateral expansion into China and Southeast Asia so as to strengthen the nation; and, third, the pro-Western idealistic stance that rejected power politics and argued that Japan should make a contribution to peace, morality, and democracy. The last two positions were critical of the government's cautious diplomacy of imperialism.

Attacking what they took to be the government's passivity, some critics argued that Japan must seek positive cooperation with China, while others asserted that the nation should establish a leadership position there. The former, represented for instance by Tōa Dōbun-kai (the Society for Asian Solidarity), stressed the need for Chinese–Japanese cooperation; Japan, the society insisted, must take the initiative to preserve Chinese integrity so that the two nations would work together for the peace of Asia. The latter view, in contrast, argued that Japan should not be so concerned about Western reaction but should act assertively to establish its position as 'the leader (*meishu*) of East Asia'.

Kokuryūkai (the Black Dragon Society) members tended to stress such a perspective. Both viewpoints had in common the assumption that there was something special about Japan's relations with China, and that the East should hold its own against the West. Both, therefore, espoused pan-Asianism, equally denouncing the government's 'realistic' foreign policy and refusing to accept the need to accommodate Japan into the currents of international politics in which Western policies and precepts dominated. There were images of 'Asia' and 'the West' that were supposed to be fundamentally different from, even diametrically opposed to, one another. Japan, in such a perception, belonged to Asia, and it was its mission to resist the West's penetration of Asia and to contribute to Asia's 'awakening'. Ultimately, it was asserted, there should emerge an 'Asia for Asians' under the leadership of Japan.

Such ideas provided the ideological basis for an alternative view of Japanese foreign relations, one that was in a sense a reaction against the non-ideological nature of official policies. Okakura Tenshin, one of the ideologues of pan-Asianism, declared in 1902 that 'Asia is one'. He had studied Western art and was familiar with European languages, but he had been impressed with what he took to be Western imperialism's victimization of Asia. He came to believe that Asia was enveloped by 'an expansive force of love which seeks something ultimate and universal', qualities that set the land apart from Europe's civilization. It was a step from such a view to the insistence that Indians, Chinese, Japanese, and other Asians should awake to their historical legacy and recognize the sense of beauty that was common to them all; when they did so, they would be able to liberate themselves from the West's cultural influence and be able to regain their self-confidence so that they would once again be able to contribute to the world's civilization. Such thought reflected a desperate search for some philosophy of foreign affairs which the government seemed incapable of providing.

Obviously, the East and the West as stipulated by pan-Asianist thought did not correspond to the realities of either. Neither East nor West as a cultural entity existed in immutable form and, besides, ideas and life-styles in the West were rapidly changing at the turn of the century. The pan-Asianists' West was little more than 'the West' that they imagined, or that they wanted to imagine, in either instance a product of subjective thinking. Their 'West' had little to do with the actual West but was a product of the supposition that Asia had to be liberated from the West, or that Japan must become Asia's leader. There was an image of East–West relations that had widespread appeal to Japanese people, but here again such a dichotomy was more a reflection of Japan's own intellectual trends and political conditions than of the actual relationship between Eastern and Western countries. Nevertheless, it is important to recognize that the appearance of pan-Asianist rhetoric at this early stage provided an intellectual underpinning for the sense of dissatisfaction with official foreign policy that was being felt by the Japanese. The one represented Japan's idealism, and the other realism, in the conceptualization of the nation's foreign affairs.

Interestingly enough, the East–West dichotomy was also being popularized outside Japan. After 1890, scholars and journalists in Europe and North America showed an unusual interest in the phenomenon of Asia's Westernization and expressed their views on the future of East–West relations that were more often than not quite alarmist, even fatalistic. It was believed that the progress of science and technology would in time affect Asian countries so that they, hitherto 'asleep', would finally awaken and initiate their own programmes of industrialization. The fact that in Japan, political, economic, and military Westernization had been successfully launched gave rise to much speculation among Europeans and Americans about the future of Western civilization. For if Asia were to Westernize, this might challenge the West's position of superiority in the world. Would a Westernized Asian civilization be still different from Western civilization? If so, would such an Asia retain an anti-Western orientation? The most pessimistic answer to such questions took the form of the 'yellow peril' doctrine, asserting that Asians, who lacked a spiritual civilization comparable to the West's, would be a formidable threat to the West's position in Asia once they adopted modern technology and undertook superficial Westernization. Such fatalism became rather widespread in the 1890s. Of course, it cannot be said that a hysterical yellow-perilism dominated Western perceptions of Asia at that time. The fact that the powers did not openly oppose Japan's development as an imperialist suggests that they were not really alarmed over Japan's joining them as one of the great powers.

Nevertheless, it cannot be denied that there was an undercurrent of concern over the future of East–West relations in the writings of leading thinkers at that time. Captain Alfred Thayer Mahan, for instance, one of the foremost authorities on international affairs, wrote an essay in 1897, entitled 'A Twentieth Century Outlook', and noted that 'the East is rapidly appreciating the material advantages and the political traditions which have united to confer power upon the West'. Such 'a stirring, a rousing from sleep' on the part of the Orient could be a very frightening phenomenon if it were not accompanied by the West's spiritual values. If, Mahan concluded, Christianity could not influence Asians, then the West must even be willing to use military force to prevent them from trying to rule the world. As he said, 'whether Eastern or Western civilization is to dominate throughout the earth and to control its future' was the most serious problem the twentieth century was likely to face. Such fatalism could be seen in many publications at that time, no doubt inspired by Japan's successes in Westernization. There was concern over whether Japan would Westernize itself spiritually as well as materially. If not, it could choose to lead the rest of Asia against the West. Even if Japan could be seen as having been superficially modernized, to many observers it still appeared to be bound to tradition and therefore remain one of the Asian countries. Such an image of Japanese culture and history would buttress fatalistic perspectives on East–West relations.

These were some of the important intellectual currents that were enveloping Japan even as it successfully extended its influence over Korea by following an imperialistic foreign policy. These currents suggested that, despite its seeming successes, Japan faced an uncertain future. Just as Japan's pan-Asianists had rather subjective and emotional views of the West, Westerners' alarmist views of Asia or of East–West confrontation reflected their insecurity. It was as if they wanted to reassure themselves that despite Asia's modern transformation the West could retain its supremacy. Thus the image of East–West conflict which emerged at the very moment when the East was becoming Westernized indicated a psychological crisis. The image was easy to grasp and appealed to emotion, quite apart from the reality of East–West relations. For that very reason, however, these emotional and psychological trends were sure to complicate the course of Japanese diplomacy, no matter how 'realistic' it might remain.

Chapter 3

THE ROAD TO
CONTINENTALISM

It was after the outbreak of the war with Russia that Japanese leaders shifted to an assertive policy towards the China continent, going beyond the existing objectives of establishing control over the Korean peninsula and penetrating south China economically as much as possible. Now Japan was paying particular attention to south Manchuria, turning the region into a Japanese sphere of influence so that the nation would start a new career as a continental power. Precisely at that juncture, however, in China a serious movement for 'rights recovery' arose, complicating its domestic and foreign affairs. Japanese diplomacy inevitably became more complex. What the novelist Nagai Kafū said of the Japanese people's spiritual life – 'We have arrived at a moment when we must seek to understand what this "period" is in which we are living' – applied equally to the nation as a whole.

Japan's new departure was already clear in a memorandum written by Foreign Minister Komura Jutarō a mere five months after the outbreak of the war. Whereas the nation had been satisfied with maintaining the existing rights in Manchuria, he asserted, it was now necessary 'to go a step further' and 'to turn [Manchuria] to some extent into our sphere of influence in order to protect and expand our interests'. At bottom was the perception, which itself was nothing new, that 'in the recent years the great powers have been intent upon expanding their interests in the Far East', so that Japan should 'not fall behind them' but 'seize the moment and expand our interests in Manchuria, Korea, and the Maritime Province so as to augment our national power'. While such expansionist thought had existed for some time, to which little new was added in the vocabulary of Japanese imperialism, it should be noted that it was now accompanied by a sense of insecurity which was both intellectual and psychological. There were simply too many developments in the wake of the Russo-Japanese war: nationalism in China, the anti-immigration movement in the United States, the intensification of the naval rivalry, the gravity of the Balkan question, and, domestically, divisions among the political leaders, as well as the emergence of an emotional public opinion as demonstrated when a mob started burning buildings in Tokyo in protest against the terms of the peace treaty with Russia. (The treaty, signed in Portsmouth, New Hampshire, ceded Russia's rights in southern Manchuria as well as the southern half of Sakhalin island to Japan. But Russia paid no war indemnities.)

Nevertheless, there is little evidence that the leaders sought to go beyond the principles of imperialistic diplomacy: to pay the closest attention to the policies of the powers, to cooperate with them as much as possible, and to safeguard Japanese security and interests in that framework. There persisted the static image of world affairs, that the great powers were in a sort of equilibrium, and that the best course for Japan was to fit itself into the equation. In other words, it was assumed that the diplomacy of imperialism would continue to operate. Kurino Shin'ichirō, a senior diplomatist, was a strong advocate of such a stance. He was fearful of any hint that the Japanese might advance a pan-Asianist cause which, he believed, could only arouse Western suspicion and cause the Western powers to unite against Japan. If that happened, Japan's position as a civilized power would be severely compromised. Accordingly, the only policy Japan should pursue was to cooperate with Europe and America in dealing with Asian problems. As he told the French foreign minister:

It is a complete misunderstanding to think, as some apparently do, that Japan is seeking to establish its unilateral hegemony in the Far East, or that it detests foreigners and wants to work together with the Chinese. Japan is only interested in cooperating with other nations that have large interests in China and in developing the latter's commercial and industrial opportunities so as to share equally in the benefits accruing from them.

In such a perspective, international politics was still revolving around the Western powers, and the only possible framework for Japanese diplomacy remained cooperation with them. To avoid arousing their suspicion while Japan concentrated on economic development and military strengthening – these were still the principal objectives for officials such as Kurino. Foreign Minister Hayashi Tadasu (1906–08) fully agreed, terming the approach 'conservative'. To 'conserve' the existing rights and interests within the framework of peaceful, harmonious relations among the imperialist powers – that appeared to be the best course for the nation to follow.

However, not everybody adhered to such a rigid stand. Komura Jutarō, for instance, was already coming to the conclusion that the inter-power relations were constantly shifting and, therefore, that the seeming equilibrium in Asia was not likely to last. He thus opposed basing Japanese policy on cooperating with the powers, for that could lead to loss of freedom of action. Rather, Komura thought, Japan should adopt a more flexible approach in order to expand on the Asian continent and to develop its domestic commerce and industry, the basic national objectives. While he was unhappy about the army's tendency to ignore other countries' intentions in extending its power over Manchuria, he believed that continental expansion was a 'definite and immutable policy' for the nation, along with such other policies as trade expansion and emigration overseas. While he still considered it necessary to rely on Western economic resources and thus to act within the framework of imperialist foreign relations, he was willing to countenance the pursuit of a unilateral policy in Asia, to turn Japan into an Asian power. Still, he stopped short of espousing an explicitly pan-Asianist approach. As he said, Japan should 'act together with the Western nations in matters that concern all the powers ... and, at the same time, have them gradually recognize our special position in Manchuria'.

The Japanese army, on the other hand, was coming to the view that even Komura's ideas were old-fashioned and inadequate, now that Japan had decided to expand into south Manchuria. Already at the end of the Russo-Japanese war, Senba Tarō, commanding officer of the Japanese army in Tientsin, had advocated that there should be created a 'new Japan' in Manchuria through cooperation with Chinese leaders like Yüan Shih-k'ai. Aoki Norizumi, military attaché with the Japanese legation in Peking, agreed, stating that Japan should take over the defence of this region. When Japanese military forces were sent to Manchuria after the war, to safeguard the newly acquired leasehold in Liaotung peninsula and the South Manchuria Railway, they were in effect responding to such ideas. Incorporating Manchuria into the national defence system came to be known as 'Manchurian management'. It suggested a special relationship between Japan and this part of China. The nation would turn the Manchurian region into the base of its continental expansion and proceed unilaterally, regardless of the vicissitudes of international politics.

Such thinking inevitably led to an Asian-oriented expansionism. Tanaka Giichi, who as a member of the General Staff's operation section was engaged in drafting guidelines for national defence policy, was a good exemplar of this new expansionism. According to him, after the war with Russia, Japan had made it the basic policy to abandon an 'insular condition' and to become 'a continental state' in order 'to expand our national fortune'. Korea and south Manchuria were obviously an important part of the new 'continental state', but Japan must now seek to expand its influence elsewhere in China. 'Our international and geographical relationship with China is superior to those of other countries, and so it follows that we must make our national interests and rights in China superior to those of others', he wrote, adding: 'Such is our heaven-given right, an objective we must seek to attain.' In such a view, alliances and ententes with the Western powers, however important, were merely means to an end. To turn cooperation with the West into a principle of Japanese diplomacy was to prevent the freedom of action of Japan, which was by nature an Asian power. Such thinking, stressing Japan's uniqueness and Asian orientation as the guiding principle of postwar foreign policy, grew steadily inside the army.

The navy, on the other hand, was critical of such a stand and viewed international relations more flexibly. For instance, the instructions issued to the delegates as they departed for London in 1907 to negotiate a military agreement between the two allies stated: 'While the nation's position has undeniably been strengthened through our military defeat of Russia's army and navy and the extension of our alliance with Britain, these have also contributed to destroying an equilibrium among the great world powers. The result is that international affairs are still in a state of confusion.' The 'Guidelines for our national defence', adopted by the Japanese leaders in 1907, still viewed Russia as the primary hypothetical enemy, but the navy added to the list France, an ally of Russia's, and the United States, fast expanding its naval presence in the Pacific. But these guidelines were not static, and the Japanese navy believed that in order to cope with the 'confusion' in world affairs, it was necessary to be prepared for a global war which might obliterate the existing alliances and hypothetical antagonisms. The best way to prepare for such an eventuality, it was reasoned, was to augment Japan's own naval power, especially since all major powers appeared to be doing so, as witness their rapid construction of *Dreadnought*-type warships. Ultimately, Japan's naval planners dreamed of constructing three 'eight-eight fleets', each consisting of eight battleships and eight cruisers. In thus stressing Japan's maritime defence, the navy was contesting the army's emphasis on the continent. Rather than defining Japan as a continental state, the navalists characterized the nation as a maritime power whose peculiarity lay in its insular nature. Hence the importance of coastal defence and the augmentation of naval strength. To expand indiscriminately into the continent, they argued, was to ignore these needs closer home and to invite unnecessary friction with Russia and China, both continental states. The navy's expansionism was directed, not at the continent, but at the Pacific ocean, especially in the economic sphere. As Satō Tetsutarō, one of the leading naval strategists, asserted: 'We now have an opportunity to undertake global expansion, but this global expansion should take the form of maritime expansion, whether or not we consider our nation a naval or a continental state.' Such views expressed the disunity among

Japan's military as well as civilian leaders concerning the nation's future in a changing world environment. Nevertheless, it is notable that virtually all opinions at this time embraced a power-political argument, seeing international relations geopolitically, as an arena for the engagement of military force among the powers. There was assumed a power equation; since power was the key factor, international relations appeared amenable of rational calculation, although 'power' could mean ground troops to some, warships to others, and economic strength to still others.

Ironically, precisely at this moment, Japanese foreign affairs experienced some significant crises which could not be solved in the framework of power-based equations. The rise of anti-Japanese sentiments in the United States, and the growth of rights-recovery movements in China, were two important examples. Neither appeared suddenly after the Russo-Japanese war, but it was only then that they came to bedevil Japanese leaders who were accustomed to conducting foreign affairs on the basis of power-political calculations.

In the United States, there had been negative sentiments towards Japan since the last years of the nineteenth century because of the influx of cheap Japanese goods and the coming of large numbers of Japanese immigrants, but it was after the war that an organized movement arose to curb the rights of Japanese on the west coast and to bar altogether the immigration of Japanese labourers. The anti-Japanese sentiment was abetted by what American merchants took to be the unfair treatment they experienced in Manchuria under Japanese military control, often resulting in their commercial failures. There even appeared books forecasting a Japanese–American war. These incidents were sustained by a racialist perspective which combined a sense of superiority of Western civilization with an alarm over a Japan that seemed to threaten this superiority. There was an explicit cultural and racial prejudice of the kind exemplified by the remarks of Willard Straight, the consul-general in Mukden (Feng-t'ien) that 'the change [in modern Japan] has been essentially that of a man who keeps a new suit and rides a new horse – his character won't change'.

The intrusion of something as irrational as race prejudice into foreign policy considerations was a shocking development for Japanese leaders. To be sure, as noted earlier, they had long been aware of the 'yellow perilist' argument in the West, and to prevent the growth of such a sentiment, they had painstakingly tried to cooperate with the Western powers. But the anti-Japanese movement in the United States went beyond race prejudice and created diplomatic incidents, even generating some imaginary war stories. For those Japanese who had believed in the possibility and advantages of cooperating with the Western powers, these developments were quite troublesome, indicating that factors unrelated to power or economic considerations could intrude upon international relations. It is suggestive that Hayashi Tadasu, Japan's foreign minister when the California crisis arose, viewed it as essentially a temporary nuisance. Typical of those who thought in the framework of the diplomacy of imperialism, he was convinced that Japanese relations with the United States, like those with other powers, were of a military and economic nature; therefore, so long as they entertained no territorial ambitions at the expense of one another, there should be no crisis between the two nations. The crisis atmosphere was produced by some labour union leaders and journalists for some domestic reasons, Hayashi believed, but they did not represent the American people or the government. The crisis should go away once Tokyo and Washington negotiated a 'gentlemen's agreement' to restrict Japanese emigration to the United States. Hayashi did not want to make the agreement a formal document, for to do so would amount to recognizing America's right to discriminate between European and Japanese immigrants, contrary to Japan's professed goal of seeking complete equality with the powers. In other words, there was no need to go beyond the existing framework of diplomacy; he refused to recognize that irrational issues unique to certain pairs of countries, such as the immigration dispute between Japan and the United States, could not be fitted into the existing diplomacy of big-power relations. Hayashi's successor, Komura, returning to the Foreign Ministry in 1908, was likewise blind to the new forces. They cannot, of course, be blamed for the crisis itself, which was rooted in race prejudice in the United States, but the Japanese leaders' responses indicated their inability to go beyond the conventional wisdom that emotional phenomena like the immigration dispute were of minor consequence in comparison with more fundamental issues like security and trade.

Even more of a challenge to Japanese diplomacy than the immigration dispute with the United States were the developments in China which culminated in the 1911 overthrow of the Ch'ing dynasty. The dynasty began various reform efforts after the Boxer catastrophe in order to strengthen the country politically, economically, and militarily. Its foreign policy now aimed at 'rights recovery'. Simultaneously, a new 'public opinion' emerged, represented by trade associations, provincial assemblies, and newspapers and magazines. While in general supportive of the government's programmes, significant parts of China's public opinion turned revolutionary, convinced that no substantive reform would succeed so long as the Manchus ruled the country. The radicalization of Chinese politics came to a head after 1908, when both the Empress Dowager and the Kuang Hsü emperor died.

These developments provided a new challenge to Japanese diplomacy, but it was difficult to define a systematic approach to them so long as Japan was guided by the principles of power politics. To take Foreign Minister Hayashi as an example, he was clearly unprepared for the radical turn of Chinese politics and foreign affairs. But he sought to cope with the situation through the existing, status quo-oriented diplomacy of imperialist collaboration. He believed that so long as the great powers continued to cooperate, Japan's position in China would remain secure, no matter what happened on the continent. This entailed the preservation of the powers' respective spheres of influence, including Japan's in Manchuria. Even if things got out of hand in China, Hayashi thought, Japanese rights and interests would be protected if Japan could avoid becoming isolated; hence the need for continued collaboration with the powers. In such a framework, an alternative strategy, that of expressing support for Chinese nationalism and making cooperation with China the basis of Japanese policy there, was unrealistic, for, he asked, how could Japan obtain Chinese understanding when it was sitting on its privileges in Manchuria? Thus reasoning,

Hayashi saw no need to develop a new approach towards China or to define a systematic response to Chinese nationalism. When, for instance, a boycott of Japanese goods began in Canton and elsewhere in 1908 in protest against the high-handed manner in which Tokyo forced the settlement of the *Second Tatsu Maru* incident (the seizure of the Japanese ship by Chinese officials on the grounds that it was carrying arms for revolutionaries in south China), Hayashi saw the movement as tactical manoeuvring by a faction headed by K'ang Yu-wei, one of the anti-Ch'ing reformers, to embarrass the government and demanded stringent measures to suppress it. (K'ang had been supported by some Japanese eager to help promote reform movements in China. He went back and forth between China and Japan to agitate for reform, but officially the Tokyo government took no notice, nor did it support a movement aimed at overthrowing the Peking – Beijing – regime with which Japan maintained a diplomatic relationship.)

There were, however, some officials who took Chinese nationalism more seriously. Japan's minister in Peking, Hayashi Gonsuke, for instance, argued that 'the recent atmosphere in China pushing for the recovery and protection of national rights is the product of a natural sentiment that has accompanied the people's growing self-awareness'. Such a sentiment, he said, could never be suppressed by external force; Japan, therefore, should 'make use of it' and 'try to guide and direct such emotions by expressing our support for them to some extent and by making sure that the Chinese people understand our true intentions'. Japan should never give the impression that it was seeking to divide up China with the powers but rather develop 'ideas about our shared interests' in Manchuria and spread those ideas among Chinese officials and people so as to obtain their friendship. Regarding the rapidly changing political situation in China, Japan should 'try to strengthen among Ch'ing court and local leaders a greater sense of trust in us than in any other country so that our influence will be maintained even in the event of an unforeseen development'. Thus, while Foreign Minister Hayashi based Japan's continental policy on cooperation with the powers, thereby underestimating the force of Chinese nationalism,

Minister Hayashi believed that support for China's political unity and its nationalism was the best means for preserving Japanese interests.

Both officials left their respective offices in 1908, but these contrasting approaches, one realistic and the other idealistic, were never reconciled by their successors before revolution came to China in 1911. In a way the divergent approaches approximated the army–navy division of views as noted above. Compare, for instance, the army's perspective as expressed by Tanaka Giichi with the navy's as developed by Satō Tetsutarō. Tanaka wrote, 'we should be prepared to use force in China, should an opportunity present itself either because China becomes incapable of maintaining domestic order or because it encounters some complications in dealing with a foreign power. That will be an excellent opportunity for us to extend our national interests and rights so as to enable our nation to emerge as the hegemon in the Far East.' Satō, in contrast, argued: 'Our programmes in Manchuria should be peacefully and internationally [i.e. through cooperation with the powers] promoted as much as possible and should aim at eradicating difficulties in our path rather than reaping huge profits.' Obviously, these two represented divergent perspectives, but it should be noted that both viewed China as an arena for Japan's and other powers' exploitation, and that neither showed much interest in developments within the country.

These examples suggest that Japanese diplomacy in the wake of the Russo-Japanese war was characterized by conceptual confusion. This confusion can be attributed to the growing division among Japanese leaders as to how to view the nature and future of international relations, and the emergence of qualitatively new issues – such as race prejudice and Chinese nationalism – that did not easily fit into traditional precepts of diplomacy. The diplomacy of realistic, geopolitical calculations which had provided a unifying theme for Japanese leaders was giving way to unpredictable problems, just when they had brought to a conclusion such specific issues as treaty revision and control over Korea.

The feeling of uncertainty, and the consequent groping for more meaningful direction of Japan's foreign affairs, may be read in an essay entitled, 'The Melancholy of Victory', published in 1905, just after the end of the Russo-Japanese war, by a popular novelist, Tokutomi Roka. Born in 1868, the first year of the Meiji era, he had identified with the course of modern Japanese diplomacy and initially supported the war against Russia in defence of the national interest. During the course of the conflict, however, he began to develop a profound scepticism about the war and about the policies and strategies that had led to it. Although Japan's victory resulted in the acquisition of new territory (South Sakhalin) and new rights (in south Manchuria and Korea), these were nothing to boast about, in fact not 'even worth a single drop of blood'. To speak of postwar Japan's 'expansion', the novelist wrote, was nothing but meaningless 'empty talk' and 'posturing'. For nothing had really changed; the nation's independence still hinged on military power and an alliance system with the other powers, and its economy depended on tea and silk for export, south Manchuria's coal, and Taiwan's sugar and camphor. A successful resort to force might enable Japan to join the ranks of the great powers, but the Japanese should never forget that 'those who live by the sword shall perish by the sword'. Besides, they should realize that the victory over Russia had cheered the world's coloured races and, for that very reason, provoked the suspicion of the white race. The Russo-Japanese war, then, could prove to have been a prelude to the coming inter-racial conflict 'unprecedented in the annals of world history'. Thus, ironically, the stronger Japan had become, the more insecure its position had grown, causing other countries more and more misgivings. In such a situation, the nation must alter its foreign policy and redefine its role in the world fundamentally. Instead of persisting in single-minded military strengthening and territorial expansionism, it should accept the pursuit of peace as its primary mission and dedicate itself to 'spreading justice in all four seas'. The people must recognize that it was a folly, even a sin, to kill at the behest of the state and instead value 'man's deepest and most natural feelings', which were oriented towards love, peace, and humanitarianism.

Roka, who would continue to advocate these views as a leading Christian socialist and pacifist, had few followers then, but his central thesis – that Japan had 'grown, but not grown up' – was widely shared, reflective as it was of the feeling that, while the nation had successfully emulated the Western powers in certain respects, it had lost its soul, a sense of its role in the world, in short a mature self-definition. As Meiji Japan neared its end – the emperor died in 1912 – many writers besides Roka became fascinated with the question of where Japan stood in the world, whether the country and its people were any better off than during the 1850s and the 1860s, and whether they should not be doing more than just following the slogan, 'enrich the nation and strengthen the arms'.

One possible solution to such problems, and one that would be tried time and again, was to stress Japan's role in mediating ('building bridges', as some said) between East and West. For instance, Tokutomi Roka's elder brother, Sohō, a prominent journalist, wrote after the Russo-Japanese war that the nation's mission lay in 'introducing the civilizations of East and West to each other, harmonizing the relationship between the yellow and white races, and coalescing the whole of humanity so as to reach the ultimate goal of justice'. He argued that the world faced the serious question of whether East and West, the yellow and white races, would be able to accommodate one another. If not, there would be a catastrophic collision. It was, then, Japan's mission to make sure there would be accommodation, not conflict. Such a conceptual dichotomy between East and West was nothing new; Japanese (and Chinese) thinkers and officials had made use of such categories as a way of understanding world and national affairs. But some Japanese were now proposing the dichotomous scheme as the guiding principle of foreign policy. Only through such reorientation, they believed, could the feeling of uncertainty and unpredictability in international relations be overcome.

Itō Hirobumi, who was appointed first governor-general of Korea when the latter was made a Japanese protectorate in 1905, complained two years later: 'Japan's position today is most worrisome. . . . If our policies are not appropriate and if our behaviour is not proper, disaster will surely fall upon us.' Note that 1907 was the year when Japan concluded ententes with France and Russia, which, added to the alliance with Britain that was renewed in 1905, should have produced a sense of security. Instead, Itō was speaking of the nation's growing 'isolation', which he attributed to increasing anti-Japanese sentiments in the world in proportion as the nation achieved diplomatic and military successes. In other words, a high official like Itō shared the same feeling of 'melancholy' that Roka had expressed. The idea of East–West harmony as something Japan should aim at, expressed a hope, even wishful thinking, that national disaster could be averted if Japan took it upon itself to strive for better communication and understanding between the civilizations and peoples of the East and of the West. As Ōkuma Shigenobu, a prominent politician and educator who founded Waseda University, said, the two civilizations 'cannot yet be said to have become entirely harmonized, but they have almost been harmonized'. It was Japan's mission to expedite the process. The idea was appealing to those groping for some sense of direction in Japanese foreign affairs, for an escape from the growing feeling of uncertainty. There were, to be sure, sceptics about such a vision. The American-educated novelist Nagai Kafū, for instance, who said he had nothing but 'negative feelings' towards his country after the Russo-Japanese war, ridiculed his countrymen's 'superficial vanity' in indulging in a 'dreamlike illusion' like 'East–West harmony'.

Nevertheless, most Japanese who ardently spoke of the vision were really being compelled to entertain such a dream in view of the rapidly changing world. Although Nagai's scepticism was justified, as witness the further turmoil in which Japanese diplomacy was to become enveloped, the fascination with the idea of cross-cultural bridge-building has persisted to this day.

Chapter 4

JAPANESE DIPLOMACY IN TRANSITION

During the 1910s, world conditions surrounding Japan were drastically altered, bringing in their train an equally revolutionary transformation of ideas about international affairs. Every nation was confronted with the challenge of how to comprehend these changes and what concepts to develop as the new foundation of its foreign policy. Japan was no exception. Nevertheless, it is difficult to say that its diplomacy went much beyond responding to each new development in an ad hoc fashion. Japanese foreign affairs continued to be characterized by pragmatism and opportunism, without a unifying theme or comprehensive ideology in terms of which to respond to changing world conditions. However, Japanese action, however opportunistic in inception, was destined to provoke counter-action in other powers, which in turn forced the nation to respond. These series of events ultimately, towards the end of the decade, forced Japanese policy-makers to reassess the basis of their foreign policy.

To sketch briefly developments outside Japan, in 1911 a revolution broke out in China, bringing about the demise of the Ch'ing dynasty. This signalled the failure of the central government in Peking to undertake last-minute reforms and, in contrast, the growing power of the provinces, especially their 'new armies'. The drift of power to the provinces was not checked even after the revolution, although political unification should have been the major task of the revolutionaries. Yüan Shi-k'ai, the Ch'ing military leader who survived the collapse of the dynasty and emerged as provisional president of the Chinese Republic, tried desperately to reunify the country, but all he had to rely on were the armed forces under his control and the prospect of political and financial support by the foreign powers. But the powers did not have a uniform policy towards China, and some of them in fact sought to take advantage of the weakness of the republican government to expand their territorial and economic interests in the country. In time China fell under the control of local power-holders, or warlords. At the same time, however, nationalism came to play a key role in keeping the nation together. Young China, consisting of officials, journalists, and intellectuals in their twenties and thirties, most of them having been educated abroad or at modern schools at home, actively promoted the cause of the 'new China'. Insisting that, even though the country might be internally divided, externally its independence and sovereignty must be preserved, these young leaders served to give direction to a country that was seemingly in hopeless confusion. Most of them were Westernizers; in Ch'en Tu-hsiu's terms, the new China needed the West's democratic and scientific thought. The journal, *Hsin Ch'ing-nien* (The new youth), called upon all Chinese to re-create themselves, to abandon the old and develop a new state. China's foreign policy, they insisted, must reflect and promote such nationalistic opinion.

Simultaneously with these developments in Asia, the Balkan crisis and the naval race among European countries, in the context of a rigid alignment of powers (Britain, France, and Russia pitted against Germany and Austria–Hungary), brought about the summer crisis of 1914, culminating in a general European war. Their navies battled against one another in the Mediterranean and the Atlantic, their trade with other parts of the world diminished, and altogether 8.5 million youths lost their lives through four years' brutal fighting. Russia, one of the combatants, underwent a revolution in 1917 and left the war in 1918, only to invite an allied expedition to Siberia. In 1917, the United States and China entered the war on the side of Britain and its allies, with the result that China was able to abolish the extraterritorial privileges of Germany and Austria, two of the enemy states. Thus the internecine war between the imperialist powers led to the undermining of imperialism at the hands of one of the victims of imperialism. The United States, on its part, gained a decisive voice at the peace conference by virtue of having entered the war. It replaced the war-weary European countries as the most powerful and richest nation.

Even more important than such vicissitudes at the power level was the loss of confidence on the part of Europeans, as well as growing scepticism about the validity of the traditional patterns of diplomacy. Towards the end of the war, revolutionary movements grew in many countries, attacking power politics and secret diplomacy conducted by the privileged few which, they said, had resulted in such a disastrous war, and calling on democratic forces everywhere to coalesce to put pressure upon the leaders to define a new kind of peace, a peace without territorial annexations, for instance. Europe's loss of confidence was expressed in the popular theme of 'decline of the West' that was heard more and more loudly among European intellectuals, dismayed that this, the most advanced of civilizations should have become involved in a war that amounted to Europe's digging its own grave. Was anything wrong with modern science and political systems that they should have produced such a tragedy? Was European civilization destined to decline, like all other civilizations? Where could Europeans turn to recover some hope? These questions often produced extreme pessimism; sometimes they generated their opposites, hysterical self-defensiveness and exclusionist chauvinism. In either case, politicians and intellectuals alike had to admit that traditional concepts of international affairs had proved totally inadequate.

At no time was geopolitical and ideological confusion more pronounced than in the wake of the Bolshevik revolution in November 1917. Geopolitically, the collapse of the Tsarist regime meant the disappearance of Russia as an imperialist power, and the existence of a power vacuum in the Maritime province, Siberia, north Manchuria, and elsewhere to which Bolshevik authority had not yet extended. The Bolsheviks' decision to leave the war by signing a separate peace with Germany, in March 1918, caused considerable damage to British and French war efforts, preparing the ground for a Siberian expedition in the summer to relieve German pressure on the western front. Ideologically, the new regime, headquartered in

Moscow, espoused Marxism–Leninism as the basis for its foreign policy. The victory of the Bolsheviks suggested that Marxist theory could be put into practice, and Leninism, with its theory of imperialist warfare as an inevitable consequence of the struggle for markets on the part of finance capitalists, provided a new ideology of anti-imperialism. According to the new ideology, world history had reached a stage where the oppressed people in capitalist states as well as in colonial and semi-colonial areas could now look to the socialist state in Russia for support and guidance. They could work together everywhere in the world, promoting socialist and anti-imperialist revolutions so as to bring about a true peace built on social justice. The world, in such a perception, had become divided into imperialist and anti-imperialist camps, so that the European war's end would only intensify the struggle in the colonial and semi-colonial regions against imperialism. Obviously, such thought made a strong impact upon Asian countries.

To this Leninist 'new diplomacy', the United States opposed its own 'new diplomacy'. Already during the presidency of William Howard Taft, the United States had begun pursuing an assertive moralistic diplomacy, at least in East Asia, which took the form of challenging Japan's special rights and interests in China. As Taft declared: 'The national prosperity and power impose upon us duties which we cannot shirk if we are true to our ideals.' In 1912 he remarked that the nation should not long be a slave to the dogmas of the past but define a new path for the future. His successor, Woodrow Wilson, shared such thoughts, as can be seen in his famous statement: 'A nation is not made of anything physical but of its strengths and purposes. Nothing can give it dignity except its thoughts.' By America's thoughts he meant its mission to the world, the commitment to strive for humanity's peace, justice, and freedom. Clearly, here was a search for a new international order, which in turn was backed up by an idealistic image of the United States as a contributor to the task. As Wilson would insist time and again, the United States was to reject a peace defined as a balance of power and call for the establishment of an alternative system of peace that promoted the common interests of all people. This meant substituting for the status quo-oriented policies of a handful of great powers an international community based on justice and self-determination of all nations. Obviously, such a vision assumed that so long as some people were not yet free and independent, no true peace could exist, and that harmonious relations among states were possible only when the principle of national self-determination became the rule.

Such ideas have been criticized as mere rhetoric to promote capitalistic interests or as expressions of an attempt to impose America's self-image onto other countries. Some have noted the contradiction between American ideology and practice, as revealed, for instance, in Wilson's expeditions to Mexico even while espousing the principle of national self-determination. American scholars, too, have often castigated such seeming hypocrisy or the lack of realism in Wilsonian moral diplomacy. The fact remains, however, that the enunciation of these principles by the American leader during the 1910s had an enormous impact on ways in which people everywhere thought about international issues.

Both American idealism and Chinese nationalism presented major challenges to Japan's continentalism. Not only rhetorically, but militarily the United States was increasing its influence in Asia and the Pacific, especially after the Panama canal was opened in 1914. The US navy expanded rapidly during the war and established its substantial presence in the Pacific. Although historians today do not think the wartime augmentation of American naval power was aimed at Japan, there was no denying that it created a new power equation in the region, now that British and German vessels had been taken away to Europe. The US Pacific fleet, consisting of a dozen warships, confronted the Japanese navy in defence of a foreign policy that stood in the way of Japan's penetration of China. Wilsonian policy sought to encourage Chinese modernization through American initiatives, rather than letting Japan 'Prussianize' China as it had done itself. The Wilsonian international order of peace and cooperation was incompatible with Japanese domination of China; instead, it necessitated an independent, free, and truly modernized (i.e. Westernized) China. Such an idea fitted perfectly into the aspirations of the Young China leaders. They – China's young intellectuals and officials – avidly turned to Wilson as a saviour to resist Japanese pressure.

Despite such challenges, by and large Japan's response during the 1910s lacked coherence and consistency. For instance, the army saw no need to redefine its existing strategy. The military leaders believed that the 1911 revolution in China made the continental strategy all the more essential and pressed the government to authorize the addition of two divisions. A memorandum written by the War Ministry's military affairs bureau three days after the outbreak of the revolution suggested various alternatives: 'Should we be satisfied with south Manchuria, occupy parts of Chihli and Shansi provinces to take possession of resources in central China, control the mouth of the Yangtze so as to occupy the river's resources as well as the mines of Tayeh, or seek the cession of Kwangtung or Fukien province?' It was as if the Chinese revolution was giving Japan an excellent opportunity to expand its territory. Inspired by such thinking, the army encouraged moves for the independence of Manchuria and Mongolia. When the cabinet of Saionji Kinmochi, one of the 'elder statesmen' from the early Meiji years, hesitated about such a strategy and refused to endorse the addition of two army divisions, there developed a major political crisis, known as the 'Taishō crisis' after the reign title of the emperor who came to the throne upon the death of his father, the Meiji emperor, in 1912.

The navy, for its part, was becoming interested in the continent. Although it had been oriented towards a 'maritime strategy' and therefore shown little enthusiasm for continental expansion, in the 1910s its leaders came to support a strategy of establishing Japanese power in the western Pacific and East Asia in order to deal with the growing crisis in Japanese–US relations. For instance, a Navy Ministry memorandum, written when the above-mentioned War Ministry document was drafted, suggested the possibility of seizing Amoy and its nearby ports as bases for stationing the Japanese fleet. Such strongholds, in addition to Taiwan and the Pescadores, 'will prove useful as springboards for our future southern operations'. Moreover, the memorandum insisted, Japan should consider establishing control over railways linking Fuchow, Kiukiang, and

Wuchang, so that in time it would become possible to extend power to the Yangtze region. After the outbreak of the European war, such ideas were further expanded and made specific in order to be fitted into a new war plan being worked out, with the United States as the principal hypothetical enemy. Plans were laid for the construction of an 'eight-eight' fleet so as to facilitate 'communication between the [Japan] mainland and the continent' as well as maintaining 'the security in the South China sea'. In July 1917, Navy Minister Katō Tomosaburō told the cabinet that the United States had become a hypothetical enemy and explained:

> It goes without saying that such a war will be a very difficult one, given the disparity in the wealth of the two countries. But we must do our very best to prepare our arms for such a conflict so that, in the event of a war, we should be ready to establish our control over the East Asian waters, wait for the enemy's advance, and steadily bring the enemy to his knees.

When the Bolshevik revolution took place in late 1917, Japan's army and navy both sought to respond to the situation by extending Japanese influence to the Maritime Province and to eastern Siberia. As a navy memorandum noted, a unilateral military expedition to Vladivostok would serve to prevent foreign intervention, especially American designs in Siberia, and 'prepare the ground for establishing our advantageous position in the future'. Just as the navy was thus trying to extend its sphere of action northward, the army wanted to take advantage of Russia's internal disunity and disorder by detaching Manchuria, the Maritime Province, and eastern Siberia from both Russia and China so as to establish a neutral area. These steps, it was asserted, would serve to ensure the security of the Japanese empire. Although an expedition to Siberia, undertaken in August 1918, was nominally carried out in cooperation with the United States, Japan acted unilaterally in most instances, its forces occupying strategic areas in north Manchuria and the Maritime Province. In the meantime, the army signed a military agreement with the Chinese government headed by General Tuan Ch'i-jui, designed to increase Japanese influence over the warlord regime in Peking.

It should also be noted that changes in international relations during the 1910s had important economic implications for Japan. Prior to the outbreak of the European war, Japan had not fully recovered from a recession in the aftermath of the Russian war, and some commentators had even argued that Japan's colonial enterprise would need to be scaled down to save money. All this changed, however, as signs of economic expansion began to appear in just a few months after August 1914. Whereas the nation's capital accumulation had been well behind the Western powers', and it had not been able to compete with them successfully in expanding its trade and investment opportunities in China, the war changed the picture completely. Thanks to the virtual cessation of European–Chinese trade, Japanese exports to the continent grew rapidly, and Japan became a creditor nation for the first time in modern history. Tokyo sought to seize the moment to entrench Japanese economic power in China. A good example was the 'twenty-one demands' imposed on Peking in 1915, which included demands for new rights in Manchuria, Shantung province, and the Hanyehping coal mines in central China. In 1918, moreover, there were additional agreements on Shantung and elsewhere. Together, these agreements sought to ensure Japan's penetration of the China market and otherwise to establish a special position on the continent while Europe's economic power weakened.

It would be wrong to say, however, that Japanese economic policy during the 1910s was focused on continental expansion and had an inherently anti-Western orientation. Japanese trade and investment were no more directed at the continent exclusively than in the immediate aftermath of the Russo-Japanese war. Particularly notable was the growth of economic ties with the United States. During the Great War, Japan's exports to the United States quadrupled, and imports from it increased five-fold. Japanese industry which had tended to turn to Britain as the main source of capital now shifted its attention to American funds. Many recognized that the future of the Japanese economy hinged on close ties with the United States and called for a friendly diplomatic relationship with the latter, no matter what the state of the two nations' military relations. Even the cabinet of General Terauchi Masatake, which promoted an expansionist continental policy in the second half of the war period, pursued a policy of 'establishing a permanent and firm friendship between Japan and the United States'. Such a policy necessitated that even in China, where America's economic activities were being pursued with great vigour, Japan should not interfere with them 'so long as our own special interests are not jeopardized'. There was hope that capitalists in the two countries might join their resources together for the development of China. Governmental leaders such as Hara Kei, head of the Seiyūkai party who became prime minister in 1918 in what constituted the first party cabinet in Japanese history, and Shidehara Kijūrō, a high Foreign Ministry official, were coming to the view that the maintenance of close economic links with the United States was the most crucial objective for Japanese foreign policy. Hara, in particular, adopted an explicitly cooperative policy towards the United States, believing that such cooperation (whether to be undertaken in China, in Siberia, or elsewhere) would bring peaceful pursuits of economic interests to the core of Japanese diplomacy. The military's emphasis on forceful expansion, in contrast, would lead to friction and conflict with the United States and other powers, not to mention being a waste of national resources, and must therefore be resisted. This was because, according to Hara and his colleagues, the expansion of economic interests could best be promoted through a policy of international cooperation.

The trouble was that there was no easy reconciliation between these divergent policy alternatives. In particular, the gap between Japan's military and economic policies could not be filled without some serious rethinking about the nature of the national interest, which in turn necessitated mature deliberations on the future of the country and of the world. Whereas prior to the Russian war the gap had been narrow, because there had been an essential consensus about the need for modernizing Japan in a world dominated by the imperialist powers, there was now greater conceptual ambiguity.

On the one hand, pan-Asianist thought grew during the early Taishō period, becoming more exclusionist, tending to the idea of 'destroying the white tribes', in the words of Tokutomi Sohō. Such extreme thought was a reaction against the late Meiji era's emphasis (which Tokutomi himself had advocated) on harmonizing East and West. Pan-Asianism also was a rationalization for the more assertive continentalism of the new era. In either case, there was a strong mistrust of the Western powers, a paranoic view that these powers, on their side, harboured suspiciousness towards Japan. Some of the paranoia seemed justified in view of the continued moves in the United States against Japanese immigrants or the appearance of racist books with sensational titles such as *The Rising Tide of Color* and *The Passing of the Great Race*. Moreover, the Wilson administration's critical stance towards Japanese policy in China, the lack of Japanese–British cooperation during the Chinese revolution, or the absence of a concerted approach on the part of the powers towards the Yüan Shih-k'ai regime, all convinced some Japanese that there was a fundamental incompatibility between East and West. A few even asserted that it was Japan's mission to liberate Asia from the whites' domination and to carry out an 'Asian Monroe doctrine'.

The perception that the West was treating Japan unfairly, and that therefore Japan was justified in expanding into Asia, was widespread among important segments of the population. The army's Tanaka Giichi, for instance, asserted that Japan and China must cooperate against the West 'in order to establish an impregnable position'. The navy's Katō Kanji, on his part, argued that 'the Yamato race is destined to emerge as the saviour of East Asia'. In 1916, a huge public gathering on Japan's China policy adopted a resolution, stating in part: 'In these days, when the world is in chaos, peace in the East can only be safeguarded by the Japanese empire.'

Such ideas were not limited to the war years. The theme of East–West conflict, for instance, which Yamagata Aritomo reiterated in 1914 to warn his countrymen that the white race was sure to unite again once the war was over to resume its offensive in Asia, led Japanese leaders to consider the League of Nations an instrument of the Western powers to continue to dominate the world. The failure of their leaders at the Paris peace conference to adopt Japan's proposal, with China's backing, that a 'racial equality' clause be inserted in the League's covenant similarly impressed the Japanese that East and West remained as intractably opposed to one another as ever. Konoe Fumimaro's famous essay, 'Reject the British-US-centered peace', which the young nobleman penned during the peace conference, was another excellent example of pan-Asianist thinking. He argued that the so-called 'peace' being proposed at the Paris conference was nothing but the maintenance of the status quo that served the interests of the Anglo-American powers. Peace, justice, and similarly nice-sounding words, Konoe wrote, were designed to preserve and expand the interests of the Western powers' 'economic imperialism'. It was nothing but dogmatic selfishness for these powers to try to impose such ideas on the rest of the world. Although there was more to such thinking than an assumed conflict between East and West – it may be noted, for instance, that Konoe's ideas foreshadowed the post-Second World War dichotomy between advanced and underdeveloped countries – there is little doubt that here was a logical culminating point of pan-Asianist thinking in that it justified the coloured races' challenge to a global status quo which was seen as the product of the most powerful and the richest of Western countries, Britain and the United States.

At the same time, however, others continued to stress the importance of cooperation with the Western powers. Foreign Ministry officials tended to that view in contrast to the military who stressed pan-Asianism and unilateral diplomacy. Many civilians believed that in order to protect Japanese interests in China and elsewhere, it was still crucial to obtain the understanding of the great powers. That such ideas remained influential may be seen in a cabinet decision regarding Japan's response to the 1911 revolution in China. 'In Manchuria we should act together with Russia in order to protect our interests', the cabinet decided, 'while at the same time accommodating the feelings of the Chinese so as to induce them to trust us.' Towards Britain, the document continued, 'we should never waver in our adherence to the spirit of the alliance'; towards France and other countries with interests in China proper, Japan should aim at 'harmonious' relations; and with respect to the United States, 'we should try to bring it into our circle of friends as much as possible'. Cooperation and accommodation with the powers were still to be the guiding principle of Japanese diplomacy. The specific content of big-power cooperation inevitably underwent change; for instance, with Russia new agreements were signed to define their respective spheres of influence, and during the war Japan sought to have the allies recognize the rights and the lands it was acquiring from Germany. (Japan declared war on Germany in late August 1914, nineteen days after its ally, Britain, had done so, and occupied Shantung province in China, Germany's sphere of influence. In addition, Japanese forces seized German insular possessions in the Pacific: the Marianas, the Carolines, and the Marshalls.) These instances still showed that Japan's basic policy orientation remained: to maintain and expand Japan's interests in Asia through cooperation with the Western powers, rather than through unilateral initiatives regardless of their viewpoints, or through Japanese–Chinese cooperation built upon an exclusionist Asianism. As Foreign Minister Motono Ichirō said in 1917: 'The rise and fall of China have never had much impact on the rising power of our empire, and whatever racial or geographical ties the two countries have, they do not necessarily interconnect their destinies.'

The Motono memorandum reiterated the need for great-power cooperation: 'Except in certain areas of China where we have special interests, we should continue to cooperate with the powers and try to have them gradually recognize our superior position.' The memorandum was adopted by the cabinet as an official policy, indicating that as late as 1917 traditional diplomatic thinking remained influential. To cooperate with the powers so as to have them recognize Japan's special interests and spheres of influence in China meant that Japan would be prepared to recognize their special rights in return. In other words, despite talk of the search for a new definition of Japanese foreign relations, at the official level there was as yet no departure from the diplomacy of imperialism, aiming at harmonizing relations among the imperialist powers – despite the fact that by then the United States and Russia had begun advocating a 'new diplomacy'.

Even Hara Kei, a pro-American politician and prime minister during 1918–21, was no exception. As noted earlier, his pursuit of a friendly association across the Pacific reflected an awareness of the United States' critical importance to Japan economically, but his diplomacy took the form of seeking to maintain a peaceful, cooperative relationship between the two nations through mutual recognition of their respective spheres of influence. To this end, he was willing, for instance, to express his support for an American proposal for a four-power (United States, Japan, Britain, France) banking consortium for loans to China, even though the proposal was meant to undermine Japan's unilateral loan policy, such as the so-called Nishihara loan agreement of 1918 (a secret arrangement to provide the Tuan regime in Peking with 145 million yen). Hara did initially insist on excluding Manchuria and Mongolia from the consortium's activities, but when the United States objected, a compromise was struck, whereby only certain railways in the region would be exempted. This was as good an example as any of Hara's policy of promoting international cooperation within the framework of the diplomacy of imperialism. As he noted: 'While we have maintained rather vaguely that Manchuria and Mongolia fall within our spheres of influence, the settlement of the new consortium question can be said to have brought about the powers' recognition of those spheres, so the agreement will be of real benefit for us in the future.' To cite an even more famous example, Hara was adamant during the Paris peace conference that the United States should recognize Japan's newly acquired position in Shantung and was even willing to declare that Japan would never join the League of Nations without a settlement of this question. His attitude reflected the conviction that, since Japan had made reasonable concessions on other issues, the United States should be prepared to grant Japan what it considered to be of particularly vital interest. One detects no departure here from the traditional diplomacy of imperialism.

It is all the more remarkable, then, that at a time when old-style thinking on foreign affairs was still dominant, there were newer forces in Japan that were intent on developing a novel conception of international relations. Best exemplified by Yoshino Sakuzō, a Tokyo University professor and influential writer on public affairs, an increasing number of commentators began using the term, 'the trends of the world', referring to what they considered to be a global phenomenon in which morally defined and peacefully oriented relations among nations, buttressed by tides of individualism and constitutionalism at home, appeared to be replacing the diplomacy of geopolitics. Yoshino, to be sure, had in mind domestic developments among the Western democracies so that for him 'the trends of the world' were primarily those in Britain, France, the United States, and other democratic states. But he was willing to generalize from their example and to try to define a new concept of international relations, a concept that replaced military and political rivalries among states by economic interdependence and substituted the pursuit of ordinary citizens' well-being for that of traditional national interests as the basic national objective.

Among Japan's political leaders, Saionji Kinmochi and Makino Nobuaki, the plenipotentiaries at the Paris peace conference, were willing to listen to the new voices. Makino, in particular, quickly recognized that 'the old-fashioned diplomacy' was being replaced by a 'new-style diplomacy' and agreed that it was 'a world-wide trend' to embrace a diplomatic formula that was based on 'openness and fairness' and emphasized 'justice and humanitarianism'. Japan, he believed, must now identify itself with such a trend. Thus both he and Saionji insisted that the nation should join the League of Nations even if it had to make concessions on the Shantung question. The Hara cabinet, however, was not ready to go that far, and remained adamant on Shantung. The result was, as Horiuchi Kensuke, a diplomat in Paris, observed, Japan gave the impression that it was 'preoccupied only with issues that were of immediate interest to it'. Although the nation won the Shantung dispute in Paris – President Wilson gave in to Japanese demands in order to obtain Japan's membership in the League of Nations – its imperialistic policy provoked fiercely nationalistic responses in Asia, as exemplified by the March 1 uprising in Korea and the May 4 movement in China, both taking place in 1919 to protest vehemently against Japanese imperialism. Nevertheless, the fact that at least some political and intellectual leaders in Japan were embracing the spirit of the new diplomacy suggested that the nation's foreign policy might finally be ready for reformulation.

Chapter 5

THE SEARCH FOR A NEW ORDER

The main challenge facing Japanese diplomacy after the World War was how best to define its ideological foundations now that the old diplomacy of imperialism was giving way to novel approaches being promoted by the United States, Russia, China, and other countries. The nation would continue to face traditional, 'realistic' issues such as national security and trade expansion, but even these would have to be put in a new conceptual framework. How such reconceptualization would be undertaken, and how to use the new ideas in coping with the changing situations abroad, were to be among the key challenges of the 1920s.

To consider these challenges, it will be helpful to focus on the career and thought of Shidehara Kijūrō, a professional diplomat who in many ways exemplified the promise as well as the problems of Japanese foreign affairs in the postwar decade. Vice-minister of foreign affairs during the war and ambassador to the United States during 1919–22, Shidehara served as foreign minister in 1924–27 and again in 1929–31. He recognized the need for redefining the approach and objectives of Japanese foreign policy, now that its security, economic, and ideological aspects had become fractured and disunited. As a civilian diplomat, he had long opposed the military's unilateral expansionism and supported Prime Minister Hara's policy of cooperation with the powers. But, as seen above, there was nothing unusual about such a stance, which hardly went beyond the traditional framework of big-power diplomacy. But starting with the Washington conference of 1921–22, convened to discuss naval and Asian problems, Shidehara, and through him the Japanese government, came to adopt a new guideline, a new framework for diplomacy that came to be known as 'the Washington system'. This referred to the sum of all the treaties and agreements signed at the Washington conference. Included were the five-power (the United States, Britain, Japan, France, Italy) naval disarmament treaty, the four-power (the United States, Britain, Japan, France) treaty for mutual consultation that was to replace the Anglo-Japanese alliance, and the nine-power treaty signed by these and other nations, including China, for protecting the latter's territorial and administrative integrity as well as for promoting the open door. Even more important than these specific agreements was the spirit that greeted their signing. Shidehara was deeply impressed that here, for the first time, a new structure of Asian and Pacific international affairs appeared to have been established. Thus the 'Washington system' became the point of departure for Shidehara's foreign policy.

For Japan, to participate in the 'Washington system' meant that its foreign affairs were regaining a sense of unity; Japan's foreign military, political, and economic relations were once again to be integrated, rather than being pursued independently of one another. In the military sphere, the navy minister, Katō Tomosaburō, fully supported the Washington naval limitation agreement. He had been an advocate of preparedness against the United States during the war and had promoted a naval construction programme in order to prepare for such a war and to establish Japan's predominant position in the western Pacific. But he now recognized that it was unlikely that Britain, although an ally, would come to Japan's assistance against the United States. In such a situation, Japan would have to continue to spend enormous sums of money to keep up with America's naval building programme. Besides, an expanding Japanese navy might even provoke Britain to seek an alliance with the US navy. For all these reasons, Katō reasoned, it would make sense to refrain from what surely amounted to an indefinite naval arms race with the United States, and instead to preserve some sort of balance of power in the Pacific and to agree to mutual arms limitation. That would be advantageous to Japan militarily and economically, enabling the nation to divert its resources to other ends. Thus, even though the naval disarmament agreement gave Japan an inferior ratio of 3 to America's and Britain's 5 (in terms of the tonnages of their respective warships), he supported it in order to avoid war with the United States. A Japanese–American war 'is impossible', he asserted, particularly since future wars would surely involve the whole resources of nations, a situation in which Japan's inferiority to the United States was obvious. As he said, 'military power alone is not going to be enough from now on. No matter how well prepared we may be militarily, this will be of little use unless we develop our civilian industrial power, promote our trade, and develop our national resources fully. In plain language, this means that unless we have the money we cannot afford a war.' If, then, Japan were to avoid war with the United States, give up an endless naval arms race, and at the same time ensure national security, the best way would be to conclude some political accord with that country. Since, however, the United States opposed the renewal of the Anglo-Japanese alliance and resisted Japan's unilateral expansion into China, it followed that the nation should be willing to concur in the abrogation of the British alliance and accept the principle of equal commercial opportunities in China. The 'Washington system', a product of such thinking, was thus designed to avoid conflict with the United States.

Although Katō's views were not uniformly shared by the military, many of whom remained sceptical of the 'Washington system', at least to its exponents it was clear that Japan must now seek to safeguard its interests through diplomacy rather than by military means. But to Shidehara and his supporters, there was much more to the new Japanese diplomacy. It suggested a departure in Japan's foreign affairs, an acceptance of novel conceptions of international relations. Takahashi Korekiyo, who became prime minister after Hara's assassination in November 1921 by a nineteen-year-old youth – an incident which was not directly linked to Hara's foreign policy – was convinced that the Washington conference had 'achieved results that brought international relations to a new epoch and opened up new possibilities for the powers' foreign policies'. Foreign Minister Uchida Kōsai agreed, saying the success of the conference was 'an expression of the sincere hopes of people everywhere for the establishment of permanent world peace'. The trends in the world, he continued, 'demonstrate that nations are joining one another in abandoning exclusionist selfishness, promoting international cooperation for justice and peace, and endeavouring through their cooperation to achieve the goal of humanity's coexistence and coprosperity'. Shidehara himself had stated, during the Washington conference, that 'the competition for naval arms which destroys national welfare and harms international peace has become a thing of the past'. When he became foreign minister in 1924, he declared that 'the age of geopolitical manoeuvrings and aggressive policies is now over, and diplomacy has begun marching the path of justice and peace'.

While highly abstract, such expressions were not all empty rhetoric, as can be seen in some specific instances of Japanese foreign policy after the Washington conference which reflected the nation's new thinking on international affairs. For instance, Japanese leaders frequently reiterated their determination to base their foreign policy on the principle of 'international amity and unity', to promote peace and justice, not self-centred, aggressive goals. There was a sense of history behind such thought, a recognition that international affairs were entering a new epoch. This sense of history was, unfortunately, not destined to last long, but in the meantime it underlay the government's policy decisions and pronouncements. In the 1920s, it was buttressed by a foreign policy that emphasized economic objectives. Since national security was now to be safe-guarded through naval disarmament and other cooperative arrangements with the powers, Japan's energies and resources could best be devoted to economic needs. Time and again it was stressed that the source of national power was ultimately economic, and that the preservation and expansion of economic opportunities abroad was the best way to promote national interests. Such views, which constituted the 'economic diplomacy' of the time, derived their inspiration from the idea of economic interdependence as a precondition of peace, an idea that went back to nineteenth-century Europe, and even further back. It is interesting to note that the 'new diplomacy' of the 1920s was thus a direct descendant of an idea whose existence preceded the age of imperialism. In a way, classical economic thought was being utilized to underline the newness of postwar international relations. In any event, the Japanese translated such perspectives into their language of 'coexistence and coprosperity' and made it the basic framework of their foreign affairs.

Shidehara was intent on conducting his diplomacy in such a framework, identifying Japan with what he considered to be the trends of the times, promoting the nation's economic interests through peaceful means, bridging the gap between military and economic policies, and elevating the concept of coexistence and coprosperity to the status of the new principle of Japanese foreign policy, to replace the earlier preoccupation with imperialism, on one hand, and with the conflict between East and West, on the other.

How successful was the Shidehara diplomacy? We know that it was forced to retreat when the Manchurian crisis erupted in 1931, ushering in yet another period of Japan's territorial aggrandizement through the use of force. But was this ultimate failure attributable solely to Japan's 'militarism', or were there problems with his approach? Or, was the basic trouble the international environment surrounding Japan? We can discuss these questions by citing several specific examples.

Regarding Japan's relations with the United States, it was ironic that almost as soon as he became foreign minister in 1924, Shidehara had to cope with the immigration crisis, a product of the Congressional enactment of a law which explicitly forbade Japanese immigration. Shidehara, however, refused to be overly agitated, considering the issue a domestic matter for the United States. To exaggerate the crisis and damage Japanese–US relations was unwise, he believed, in view of the critical economic ties between the two countries. Likewise, Shidehara was an ardent supporter of the London naval agreement of 1930 which put a limit on the construction of 'auxiliary craft' such as light cruisers and submarines. Although the navy insisted that such restrictions compromised the nation's strategic requirements, Shidehara was willing to give priority to the maintenance of a friendly relationship across the Pacific because of the United States' overriding economic importance to Japan. For taking such a stand, he was condemned by navy hard-liners and right-wing civilians for caving in to American pressure.

Towards China, Shidehara advocated a non-interventionist policy with the cooperation of the United States and Britain. In view of the complex political situation in China, he argued, the powers should 'support and understand the Chinese people's efforts for peace'. Japan, in particular, must avoid arousing the suspicion of other countries. When anti-imperialistic nationalism came to dominate Chinese political affairs during 1924–27 – in 1924 the Nationalists and Communists formed a united front, and in 1926 their combined forces began a 'northern expedition' to unify the country – the Japanese foreign minister called on the powers to cooperate to protect the lives and property of their nationals in China through diplomatic, not military, means. He was even willing to evacuate Japanese from the interior of the country to avoid trouble. When Chinese and foreigners clashed, resulting in the death and injury of several foreign residents, as happened in Shanghai in 1925 and Nanking in 1927, he sought to work closely with American and British officials so as to avoid harsh retaliatory measures and to bring about a diplomatic solution of the incidents.

Shidehara acted in such a moderate manner, in sharp contrast to Japan's earlier proclivity to use force unilaterally, fundamentally because he was convinced this was the best way to promote Japan's economic interests. For him the expansion of trade and investment was the foundation of Japan's China policy. Now that the dangerous naval race with the United States had come to an end, he believed, the nation had the opportunity to define its foreign affairs primarily in economic terms. This was a diplomacy of economic rationalism, and China was to be an important testing ground for such an approach. For this reason, while he eschewed the use of force, Shidehara did not hesitate to calculate coolly Japan's economic interests and to insist on their protection and development in negotiating with the Chinese.

This can best be seen in his policy towards Chinese tariffs. The powers, Japan included, recognized that so long as Chinese politics remained chaotic, opportunities for foreign trade would be limited. One way to put an end to political instability was to strengthen the financial basis of the central government, but this could only be done if the Peking regime were granted some increases in import duties; by treaty the foreign powers had to authorize any increase over the uniform 5 per cent duty on all imports. Moreover, nationalistic Chinese were clamouring for an end to all 'unequal treaties', including the tariff arrangements, so that the powers would need to show their goodwill by agreeing to modify the tariff rates. The Peking tariff conference, convening in 1925 in accordance with an agreement at the Washington conference, provided such an opportunity. But Shidehara was adamantly opposed to unconditional tariff revision. According to him, since the bulk of Japanese imports into China consisted of cotton textiles, if import duties were uniformly raised, these textiles would no longer be able to compete with China's domestic products. Furthermore, many Japanese loans, of which the wartime Nishihara loans constituted an important part, had remained unpaid. In Shidehara's view, before China was allowed to raise its tariffs and use the new customs revenue as security for obtaining additional loans, it should be required to pay back the existing debts. Otherwise, it would become very difficult to encourage Japanese investment and loans in China. Shidehara thus insisted that certain conditions must be levied on China before the powers agreed to tariff revision: a tax should be imposed on China's domestic products; Japanese textiles and other inexpensive commodities should be subjected to lower tariffs than on imports from other countries; and a portion of the increased customs receipts should be earmarked for repaying the existing debts.

These issues were so crucial to Shidehara's economically oriented diplomacy that he was even willing to sacrifice international cooperation to achieve his ends. During the Peking tariff conference, for instance, when the United States and Britain proposed to raise the uniform import duty to 7.5 per cent, a 50 per cent increase, the Japanese delegation urged the foreign minister to accept the proposal, asserting, 'it will be extremely foolish to abandon the spirit of cooperation with the United States because of this issue'. But Shidehara refused to give in, and the conference accomplished little. Later, when the Peking government proposed that the existing treaty of commerce between the two countries should be revised, looking towards the reversion of tariff autonomy to China, Shidehara once again stood his ground. Yoshizawa Kenkichi, Japan's minister in Peking, urged him to reconsider, arguing, 'it is important to show some understanding of the hopes held by relatively moderate people in China, especially when these hopes appear to be entertained by the entire population'. But Shidehara was not persuaded. He may not have shared Yoshizawa's sanguine view of China's 'moderates', but more fundamentally he resisted any move that could possibly jeopardize Japanese economic interests in China. A Foreign Ministry memorandum written at that time reflected Shidehara's thoughts: 'While we do support the speedy realization of China's national aspirations, our ultimate goal is to promote Chinese–Japanese economic cooperation so as to protect our trade in China and to ensure the economic expansion of our citizens in China.'

Shidehara left his office in April 1927 when the cabinet headed by Wakatsuki Reijirō resigned, due to circumstances that had more to do with a domestic banking crisis than with policy towards China, but he returned to the Foreign Ministry in July 1929, to remain at the helm until just after the Manchurian incident of September 1931. There was little change in Shidehara's stance on Chinese tariffs and other economic issues. Nishi Haruhiko, who served under him in the Foreign Ministry's commerce bureau, recalls how uncompromising Shidehara was regarding such questions. He applied his economic diplomacy even to Manchuria, where he persisted in opposing a Chinese scheme to build a railway to run parallel to the South Manchuria Railway, considering such a project detrimental to Japanese economic interests. As he told Ch'en Yu-jen, a prominent Chinese official, in August 1931: 'Some of the rights we enjoy in Manchuria are inexorably linked to our nation's existence, and no matter how generous a policy we take towards China, these rights can never be given up.'

Despite such an adamant posture, Shidehara failed to persuade the military and many other critics and sceptics to his way of thinking. Despite the agreements signed at the

Washington conference, many of Japan's military leaders continued to view national defence as the key to foreign affairs. They drew up war plans against the United States and the Soviet Union, and they refused to believe that the world had entered an era of genuine peace and international cooperation. On the contrary, they were convinced that another war was likely, and that it would be a 'total war', requiring the mobilization of the nation's entire resources. In such a situation, they reasoned, it would be foolish to base Japanese security on some faith in international cooperation, economic interdependence, or the 'Washington system'. Instead, an increasing number of military officers argued, Japan must revert to unilateralism, carry out major reforms in its domestic and external affairs, and prepare for the next war by establishing control over Manchuria and Inner Mongolia so as to create a condition of self-sufficiency. The resources of Manchuria and Mongolia were of vital importance for national defence, and if nationalism in China threatened the region, Japan should be prepared to act resolutely to protect its rights.

The advocates of these views ridiculed Shidehara's optimism that Japan need not contemplate war with the United States, the Soviet Union, or China, and resurrected the earlier image of international affairs as being in a state of perpetual rivalry among nations. In the 1920s, moreover, they became particularly alarmed that both the United States and the Soviet Union, the two principal hypothetical enemies, had vastly wider spaces and richer resources than Japan. As Matsui Kuranosuke, an army officer, insisted in a book he published in 1924, entitled *The People's Primer for National Defence,*

> There are those who espouse internationalism and advocate universal love and humanitarianism, thereby belittling patriotism in order to avoid war. . . . While not lacking in beauty, such words are merely a scholar's dream and a diplomat's rhetoric. They are of little use in a real world in which nations endowed with abundant space and rich resources but sparsely populated refuse to treat other people equally, no matter how diligent and honest they are. Not only this, but such nations continue to maintain a large army and navy. If a small nation

should adopt such an academic doctrine, it is only court-
ing future trouble.

Obviously, the author had in mind the fundamental
antagonism between Japan and the United States and was
implying that in order to cope with the situation Japan must
act decisively in Manchuria and Mongolia. From such a
point of view, Shidehara's advocacy of friendship with the
United States and his emphasis on the need for political
understanding and economic interdependence with it made
little sense.

The military were not the only ones who criticized
Shidehara's approach. The 1920s saw growing national
concern with the protection of 'Japanese rights in
Manchuria and Mongolia', and many developed a 'scientific'
study of the subject. Sata Kōjirō, a researcher with the South
Manchuria Railway, gave a lecture in January 1931 under
the title, 'A scientific approach to our Manchurian-
Mongolian policy', and castigated 'the peace idea' as
nothing but 'a fool's idle dream'. Because, he said, 'natural
endowments differed from country to country', Japan,
which lacked resources, must obtain 'absolute freedom of
economic activity in the Four Eastern Provinces [Manchuria
and Inner Mongolia]'. The only way for a country like Japan
to survive, given its limited space and increasing population,
was to turn itself into 'a super-great power', and this
required the acquisition of more 'territory or at least
something with equivalent value'.

As noted above, Shidehara, too, recognized the
importance of Manchuria and Mongolia, but he wanted to
protect Japanese interests in the region through peaceful
means, convinced as he was that the world's resources could
be equitably redistributed through rational economic
means. Sata obviously did not share Shidehara's economic
rationalism, and, as the decade wore on and Chinese
nationalists embraced a 'revolutionary diplomacy' to
demand the retrocession of Dairen, Port Arthur, and other
rights earlier ceded to Japan, Sata's views, rather than
Shidehara's, came to seem more persuasive. It was
unfortunate for Shidehara that, even as he persisted in his
economically oriented foreign policy, the world-wide
Depression that began in 1929 came to undermine the

entire structure of economic internationalism. For someone like him, who had put his faith in the economic interdependence of nations, and especially in continued trade, investment, and other transactions between Japan and the United States as the key to national well-being, the Wall Street crash and the subsequent crisis of American and European capitalism were nothing short of an unmitigated disaster. Soon the idea of international cooperation would come to look like a faded dream.

Tanaka Giichi, by then a retired army general who had entered politics and headed a political party, succeeded Wakatsuki as prime minister during 1927–29. He may be considered as someone who traversed the two positions represented by Shidehara on the one hand and Sata on the other. Tanaka's foreign policy (he appointed himself foreign minister) did not differ much from his predecessor's in its emphasis on economic objectives. For instance, Tanaka agreed with Shidehara on the Chinese tariff issue and followed Shidehara's overall commitment to promoting Japanese trade and investment activities in China even as Japan agreed to discuss treaty revision with China. Part of this continuity was attributable to the fact that most Foreign Ministry officials served both Shidehara and Tanaka. Equally important, Tanaka was a strong believer in economic development and growth as the key to the promotion of national interests. Having come to power just as the nation was plunging into a serious financial crisis, triggered by the closing of small and medium-size banks, Tanaka considered the solution of the crisis his cabinet's immediate task. As he said upon becoming prime minister: 'I do not doubt that the powers will welcome our nation's appropriate economic expansion.'

It is clear, at the same time, that Tanaka did not share Shidehara's abiding faith in economic internationalism, the view that economic interdependence was the fundamental law of the international community. Nor did he think history had entered a new phase. Tanaka was much more interested in non-economic aspects of foreign affairs than Shidehara, although he was not as active a promoter of these objectives as many of Shidehara's military critics. For one thing, he was convinced that the promotion of Japan's economic interests in China was ultimately a political proposition. In view of the Nationalists' revolutionary diplomacy, the establishment of their government in Nanking, and other developments in China, Tanaka believed that the pursuit of a non-interventionist strategy or the principle of economic rationalism would not suffice. In order to protect Japanese interests in such a situation, he was much more willing than Shidehara to make use of non-economic means, including political machinations. For instance, he sought to persuade the Nationalists under Chiang Kai-shek to confine their authority to China proper; Japan would then be glad to recognize the Nationalist regime and to negotiate with it for the protection of mutual economic interests, but the Nationalists should leave Manchuria to the warlord regime of Chang Tso-lin so that Japan would be able to have its special rights safeguarded through him. Even such a scheme for separating Manchuria from China proper, however, was not sufficient from the point of view of the Japanese military in Manchuria, organized around the Kwantung Army, and some of its officers, led by Kōmoto Daisaku, succeeded in assassinating Chang in June 1928. When their conspiracy failed, and Chang's son, Chang Hsüeh-liang, assumed power in Manchuria, Tanaka sought a deal with him, offering to recognize his regime in return for his pledge to honour Japan's special position in the region. In the meantime, in contrast to Shidehara, Tanaka did not withdraw Japanese nationals from dangerous areas in China to avoid trouble but employed military means to protect them, as he did in 1927 and again in 1928 when he dispatched expeditionary forces to Shantung. Although these troops were withdrawn after the safety of Japanese nationals appeared assured, such expeditions amounted to intervening in Chinese domestic affairs, something Shidehara had scrupulously tried to avoid. Despite such interventions, the Nationalists successfully established their new regime in Nanking in 1928, and Chang Hsüeh-liang placed Manchuria under Nanking's authority.

Still, Tanaka also talked of international cooperation and was opposed to the military's emphasis on national mobilization to prepare for the next world war. In 1928, in fact, Tanaka sent Uchida Kōsai, a former foreign minister, to the United States and Britain to obtain their understanding of Japan's policy in China. It was not aimed at them, Tanaka sought to persuade Washington and London, so that the three major powers should be able to continue to cooperate there. Besides, he thought, on such other matters as arms limitation and trade expansion, the powers were in essential agreement. United States and British officials were receptive to Tanaka's overtures, and they welcomed Japan's adherence to the Kellogg–Briand pact of 1928, an international agreement to 'outlaw war'. But Tanaka resigned in July 1929, after being severely reprimanded by the emperor for his failure to mete out proper punishment to Kōmoto and others for their role in the assassination of Chang Tso-lin – one of the few instances where Emperor Hirohito (who had ascended the throne in 1926 upon the death of his father, the Taishō emperor) directly involved himself in national affairs. (The other crucial instance, of course, was his intervention in August 1945 to bring the war to a close.) Tanaka was succeeded by Hamaguchi Osachi as prime minister, and Shidehara returned to the Foreign Ministry.

In any event, in the end it was neither Tanaka nor Shidehara but the military who came to determine Japanese policy towards China. But the fact remains that during the 1920s, economic interdependence emerged as a principal idea underlying Japanese foreign policy. Because the idea would resurface after Japan's defeat in a disastrous war, it is important to locate its origins in the years after the First World War. It was unfortunate for the exponents of the idea that at that time there developed many issues that could not be dealt with within this framework. China's unification and nationalistic diplomacy were among the most serious. Neither Shidehara nor Tanaka proved as successful as the military in confronting these issues, if by success we mean the protection of perceived national interests in the short run, although the long-term damage to Japan's relations with China, and with other countries, caused by the militaristic policies was enormous.

Chapter 6

THE IDEOLOGY OF THE CHINESE–JAPANESE WAR

The year 1931, which marked the resumption of Japan's continental imperialism, came less than eighty years after Commodore Matthew Perry's visits to Japan (1853, 1854) to force the Tokugawa regime to end its policy of isolation, less than forty years after the 'unequal treaties' began to be abolished, and only twenty-odd years after the nation made its appearance on the world scene as one of the powers. In just eight decades, Japan had marched, or trotted, the distance from being in a semi-colonial situation to being a fully-fledged imperialist. This had been a history of rapid change, from one extreme to another, so that the next phase of Japanese imperialism was an integral part of that story, not something that had no relationship to the past. To understand Japan's aggression, war, and defeat during 1931–45, it is, therefore, important to put it in the context of the history of modern Japanese foreign relations, especially the ideas that lay behind Japan's external behaviour.

For instance, the Kwantung Army, resorting to unilateral military action in September 1931 – on 18 September its officers blew up a few inches of rail outside the Mukden (Feng-t'ien) station of the South Manchuria Railway and, blaming Chinese sabotage for the event, undertook military action to conquer the whole of Manchuria – was clearly conscious of its opposition to the ideas that sustained Shidehara's diplomacy. As noted already, whereas he subordinated military to economic affairs and advocated a new internationalist foreign policy fit for changing world conditions, the military rejected such an approach as unrealistic. For them, the point of departure was what they took to be the ineffectiveness of Japanese diplomacy in the 1920s and the need to restore the primacy of military, strategic calculations in the promotion of the national interest. They were nationalistic realists, opposed to Shidehara's internationalism.

And the 'realities' of world conditions in the 1930s seemed to vindicate the realists' views. For Shidehara's economic diplomacy had postulated certain 'realities' as preconditions for its success. First, there had to be an environment of relatively open and free trade relations. Second, Japan's pursuit of economic objectives should not be complicated by the intrusion of serious difficulties of a non-economic nature. Third, the domestic economy should grow steadily so that there would be no grave social problems. Fourth, as many other countries as possible should cooperate with Japan and with one another for the establishment and maintenance of a new international order. Without these 'realities', Shidehara's ideas would remain mere ideals, with few practical consequences. In the 1930s, that was what happened. The new diplomatic principles could not be carried forward in the middle of the Depression that hit one country after another after 1929. (Indeed, in Japan a recession had started two years earlier.) The powers' nationalistic economic policies in order to cope with the crisis, coupled with China's rights recovery diplomacy, undermined the rationale for economic internationalism. Japan played its part in dismantling this system by resorting to the use of force in Manchuria and seeking to establish an economic autarky, a region of self-sufficiency under Japanese control.

The Manchurian crisis clearly marked the collapse of postwar internationalism and the return to the primacy of militaristic thought in Japanese foreign policy. National defence once again became the cardinal doctrine, to which other considerations were to be subordinated. As Ishihara Kanji, a Kwantung Army officer and one of the architects of the Mukden incident, asserted time and again, national defence must be defined very broadly. As he saw it – he was influenced by German geopolitical thought, one of whose principal ideologues, Karl Haushofer, had spent some time in Japan before the First World War – the globe was becoming divided into several regions, and everywhere realignments of forces were taking place so that in time the world would come to be divided into a few blocs, each under a dominant power. In this process of 'global redivision', the powers would engage in a deathly struggle for supremacy. Each great power would have to acquire more resources, mobilize its people, and drive out other nations' economic and political influences from the region under its control. Such ideas provided the rationale for the use of force in Manchuria. As a Kwantung Army memorandum put it: 'Manchuria and [Inner] Mongolia are the strategic base for the expansion of our power.' But nationalistic Chinese – Nationalists, Communists, and virtually all others – were demanding an end to Japanese interests and influence in these areas. The only solution to 'the Manchurian–Mongolian problem', then, according to the Japanese military, was 'to turn the region into our territory'. The region's agricultural produce would be 'sufficient to solve our people's food problem', and 'its various industries will be able to make use of our currently unemployed population', Itagaki Seishirō, Ishihara's colleague, asserted. The use of force to bring Manchuria and Inner Mongolia under Japanese control, therefore, was considered imperative for preparing the nation for the next war and, at the same time, to deal with the serious economic crisis at home about which the Shidehara policy appeared helpless. In this sense, the conquest of the region was meant to serve to narrow the growing gap between Japan's economic and military policies.

Despite such determined efforts by the military, subsequent history was to show that they failed to develop a systematic strategy beyond the conquest of Manchuria and Inner Mongolia. The trouble, as Ishihara and Itagaki admitted from the beginning, was that these areas would not meet all of Japan's resource or space requirements and would therefore be 'insufficient for [the development of] a great Japan'. But what should Japan do next? There was no clear policy. Besides, Japan's unilateral action in 1931 alienated not just China but also the United States, Britain, the Soviet Union, and other nations, enormously complicating Japanese foreign affairs. Aware of the difficulties, Itagaki wrote as early as the spring of 1932 that Japan 'must be prepared to fight both China and the Soviet

Union, and even the United States together'. But to augment Japanese armed forces in order to prepare for a war on such an enormous scale would be virtually impossible, even the military conceded, and so the question of priorities inevitably arose. In other words, should Japan concentrate on conquering China, prepare for a war against the Soviet Union by focusing on the defence of Manchuria, or begin taking steps to increase naval strength in the western Pacific so as to cope with the potential threat from the United States and Great Britain? These strategies could not be pursued simultaneously, as the military became aware already during 1932–33.

In spite of such awareness, the military failed to establish any set of priorities or to develop a unified strategy. The navy regarded the United States as the major hypothetical enemy and insisted on augmenting naval power in the western Pacific, even by abrogating the naval limitation agreements signed in Washington and London. (They were all allowed to lapse in 1937, when the United States, Britain, and Japan failed to agree on mutually acceptable terms for their extension, Japan insisting on a 'parity' in naval armament with the others, and they rejecting the demand.) Ultimately, the navalists wanted to establish control over the sea lanes stretching from the China Sea to Southeast Asia. The army, on the other hand, wanted to avoid trouble with the United States while it sought to focus on preparedness against the Soviet Union. Such differences of views between army and navy were also manifest when the strategists considered options for China. The Japanese army in China sought to strengthen its position in Manchuria and Inner Mongolia by detaching north China from Nationalist control. It was also interested in forming an East Asian anti-communist bloc against the Soviet Union. The navy disagreed, however, instead insisting on a strategy of 'defending the north, expanding in the south', that is, eschewing involvement in China and increasing Japanese naval presence in Asian waters. Civilian officials – they continued to function in the bureaucracies even in this era when party politics was giving way to militaristic rule – enthusiastically supported the conquest of Manchuria which, in 1932, became the puppet state of Manchukuo. Regarding China proper, however, they preferred diplomatic means of obtaining Chinese compliance with the new status quo. As a Foreign Ministry memorandum put it, Japan should 'turn North China into an anti-communist and pro-Japan, pro-Manchukuo region, obtain resources necessary for national defence, develop railway networks, and induce the whole of China to rely on Japan and to resist the Soviet Union'.

These various opinions persisted all the way to the meeting on 7 August 1936 of the 'five ministers' (the prime minister and the ministers of foreign affairs, war, the navy, and finance) which adopted a policy paper known as 'Fundamentals of national policy'. This document, however, instead of establishing priorities among diverse strategies, merely juxtaposed them: 'Our fundamental policy towards the continent calls for a healthy development of Manchukuo, the strengthening of national defence in Japan and Manchukuo, the removal of the Soviet threat in the north, preparation for war against the United States and Britain, close cooperation among Japan, Manchukuo, and China, and Japanese economic expansion.' This was excessively broad, containing many divergent objectives, and did not lead to any definition of a unified defence policy. Of course, there was consistency in that Japanese foreign affairs were now dominated by military strategy, but precisely because of this fact, vicissitudes in the nation's strategy were perhaps inevitable, for so much depended on changing international circumstances, and the army and the navy were forced to respond to them in an ad hoc fashion.

It is hard to avoid the conclusion that, apart from their conviction that Manchuria and Inner Mongolia must be brought under Japanese control, Japan's military leaders failed to develop a consensual approach to strategy, or any systematic thought regarding the nation's position in the world. They tended to respond to each new crisis individually, without formulating long-range coherent principles and concepts. Apart from the idea of national defence, they did not produce any systematic world view or ideology of Japanese foreign affairs. Ishihara, to be sure, liked to couch his military strategy in sweeping ideological terms, which often sounded moralistic and even religious. For instance, he wrote: 'A positive [i.e. forceful] solution of the Manchurian-Mongolian problem is not only good for Japan but also for the Chinese people.' It was Japan's mission, he continued, 'to save China which has not known peace, and this is also the only way to save Japan'. This was abstract moralizing. Historians have noted the influence of Nichiren Buddhism on Ishihara's thought; Nichiren, a Buddhist monk in the thirteenth century, had adapted the religion to wide segments of Japanese society, to such an extent that the movement came to be identified with nationalism, even with the emperor worship. But apart from an ardent nationalism common to both, it is difficult to detect any connection between Ishihara's this-worldly preoccupation with Japanese defence ('Japan's road to survival') and his religious beliefs. In many instances, he was simply citing religion and morality ('our absolute faith in our nation's great ideals') to rationalize the nation's military strengthening. It is also true that Ishihara frequently referred to Japan as the main representative of Eastern civilization, pitting itself against Western civilization. There was nothing new in such a dichotomy, as we have seen. Moreover, he did not argue that such civilizational polarity inevitably led to war, that just because Japan was an Asian nation, it was fated to fight against the West. Rather, he wrote, Japan's very survival mandated that it must become 'a superpower', an objective which necessitated that Japan, 'representing the East', should make an effort to match the power of the United States, the champion of the West. Not that East and West were fated to collide, but primarily that the nation must be prepared for the coming 'real world war which will revolve around Japan'. Although he sometimes talked of racial conflict ('we must destroy the oppression by the white race that seeks to prevent us from carrying out our mission'), the starting point was Japanese defence, not inter-racial antagonism.

The Japanese government, in the meantime, was also becoming more and more influenced by Asianist thought, but Asianism was used less as a basis of foreign policy or a conceptual framework in which to view international relations, than as a justification for action already taken, mostly in an ad hoc manner. There was a rapid turnover in civilian leadership; Prime Minister Hamaguchi was wounded in November 1930 by gunshots fired by a patriotic youth unhappy over the London naval treaty of that year which assigned inferior ratios to Japan in several categories of ships such as light cruisers and destroyers; Hamaguchi was succeeded by Wakatsuki in April 1931; but the second Wakatsuki cabinet lasted only eight months, falling in December because of public criticism of its handling of the Manchurian affair. Shidehara served as foreign minister under both Hamaguchi and Wakatsuki, ardently supporting the London naval agreement and desperately trying to curb military excesses in Manchuria, but he, too, left the government in December 1931, never to return to public office till after the Second World War. In any event, till then, the Tokyo government had continued to profess its adherence to the principle of international cooperation and denied Japan's territorial ambitions, but the new cabinet headed by Inukai Tsuyoshi forsook such pretences and built its foreign policy on the basis of the *fait accompli*. Political parties and bureaucracies quickly fell into line. Thus in March 1932, the cabinet resolved that 'we should guide political, economic, security, transportation, and communications affairs in Manchuria and Mongolia in such a way as to make them an important element of our survival'. Here was clear evidence of the impact of the strategic concepts Ishihara and his colleagues had developed. Japanese leaders were once again stressing Japan's special position in Asia, asserting that it was its mission to guide China and maintain regional security. 'Our international relations have been transformed completely since the Manchurian incident', a government statement declared, indicating that the principles that had underlain diplomacy in the 1920s were no longer applicable to the new situation. Japan, therefore, would have to redefine its foreign policy, and if other countries did not recognize the new situation, the nation would have to be prepared to act unilaterally, standing firm in its resolution. That was what it did when the nation withdrew from the League of Nations in 1933. As Tokyo asserted, Japan and the League had different conceptions of 'the fundamental principles for establishing peace in East Asia'.

Japanese diplomatic thought after the withdrawal from the League can best be seen in the ideas of Hirota Kōki, a professional diplomat who served as foreign minister during

1933–36 and again 1937–38. (He was prime minister during 1936–37. Presumably because he held such key positions during the critical years of the mid-1930s, he was to be tried, and hanged, as a war criminal after the Second World War.) The so-called Hirota diplomacy aimed at forging friendly relations with other countries on the basis of the new status quo. In that sense, it was reminiscent of the diplomacy of imperialism, but this time Japan was more assertive in insisting on its unique position as the leading Asian power. A good example was his long telegram to Minister Ariyoshi Akira in Peking – the Japanese legation was not moved to Nanking, the Nationalist capital, till 1935, when it was elevated to an embassy – dated 13 April 1934, in which the foreign minister declared that Japan had a different perspective on China from other countries, and that 'we must do all we can to safeguard our mission in East Asia, regardless of whether other nations recognize this or not'. The Hirota message, which constituted the basis of what came to be known as the Amō doctrine – after Amō Eiji, the Foreign Ministry spokesman who issued a public statement outlining Hirota's ideas – stated that 'the preservation of a peaceful order in East Asia has become our responsibility which we must carry out single-handedly'. Clearly, he was building his foreign policy on the basis of what the army had carried out, so that the Hirota diplomacy was essentially diplomatic window-dressing for military action. He was even willing to insist, as the Amō statement did, that 'since China seems intent on putting pressure on us by turning to foreign powers, we must be prepared to crush all machinations on their part in China, whether or not they are undertaken cooperatively or unilaterally'. Despite such strong language, Hirota's foreign policy was known as a diplomacy of 'peace and cooperation'. Of course, this was a vastly different definition of peace and cooperation from what had prevailed in the 1920s.

For instance, Hirota proposed to the Chinese Nationalists in 1935 that they should cooperate together on the basis of three principles: the stoppage of anti-Japanese agitation in China, recognition of Manchukuo, and joint defence against communist forces. The adoption of anti-communism as an official doctrine added a new element to the vocabulary of Japanese foreign policy. Prior to 1935, Japan had viewed the Soviet Union as a hypothetical enemy and insisted that the Chinese should suppress radical anti-Japanese movements, but anti-communist ideology had not been incorporated into formal policy. From this time onward, however, the idea of Japan–Manchukuo–China cooperation 'to eject the red menace' came to be officially asserted. But this was more in reaction against the growing military power of the Soviet Union, which launched the second five-year plan in 1933 with an emphasis on national defence, than a purely ideological policy. Moreover, Japan was intent upon preventing a *rapprochement* between Nationalists and Communists in China; in August 1935 the Communists called upon the Nationalists to organize a united national front against Japan. Obviously, the Japanese were interested in stopping such an alliance and tried to persuade the Nationalists to work together with Japan against the Communists. An anti-Communist pact of Japan, Manchukuo, and Nationalist China, it was hoped, would enable Japanese forces in north China to turn northward, to prepare for possible conflict with the Soviet Union, while at the same time establishing closer political and economic ties between the two Asian countries. Likewise, at the end of 1936, Japan signed an anti-Comintern pact with Germany and Italy, also aimed at the Soviet Union. These steps, however, were more ad hoc responses to perceived changes abroad than products of some comprehensive idea. If looking for some consistent ideology of Japanese foreign affairs at this time, one would have to settle for the new emphasis on national defence. All else, from Asianism to anti-communism, seems to have been window-dressing to rationalize decisions made on the level of defence strategy.

It must also be noted that the international environment during the 1930s was such as to allow Japan to entrench itself more and more deeply on the Asian continent without strong opposition on the part of the powers. Fundamentally, this was because none of them considered their security and economic interests sufficiently threatened by Japanese action in Manchuria and Mongolia to justify countering it by force. Even the Soviet Union, perhaps the most seriously affected of the powers, was eager to focus on industrialization at home and sought to avoid trouble, going so far as to decide to sell the Chinese-Eastern Railway, built by

Russia in the 1890s to run across Manchuria, to Japan. Moscow's explicit opposition to Japanese aggression in China came only in 1935, when it called for the formation of a world-wide anti-fascist front. For Britain, its primary interests in Asia were economic, and it aimed at assisting China's financial rehabilitation without provoking Japan. The United States was initially concerned over Japan's violation of the spirit of international cooperation and considered some sanctions through the League of Nations, believing that world public opinion might induce Japan to come to its senses and to return to the peaceful conditions prevailing before 1931. Even so, American leaders did not consider the situation so serious as to justify preparing for war against Japan. For these and other countries, the primary preoccupation at that time was with domestic economic recovery, and secondarily with military strengthening, neither of which produced a strong enough stand against Japanese aggression.

To be sure, none of the powers approved of Japanese action in Manchuria, as can be seen in their support of the League's report (by the Lytton Commission) that censured Japan's use of force in Manchuria, or in their persistent refusal to recognize the puppet state of Manchukuo. But by and large these countries failed to develop an effective strategy for coping with the Asian crisis, or an ideology to sustain such a strategy. Thus, neither America's moralism nor the Soviet Union's anti-fascism was proving adequate for forging an international coalition to oppose Japan. There was a sort of international anarchy, in Asia as well as in Europe; there, too, the Western nations failed to respond forcefully to the crumbling of the postwar peace (the Versailles system) as a consequence of such episodes as the Italian invasion of Ethiopia, the German remilitarization of the Rhineland, and the Spanish civil war. The powers did not yet have a comprehensive intellectual and strategic framework in which to put these episodes as well as events in East Asia. Japan took full advantage of such circumstances, for the geopolitical and conceptual isolation of Asia fitted its designs perfectly. But the situation was about to change.

Chapter 7

THE ROAD TO THE PACIFIC WAR

On 7 July 1937 Japanese and Chinese forces clashed near the Marco Polo bridge in the outskirts of Peking. This was the beginning of a long war between the two countries, pitting Japan, intent on establishing a new order in East Asia, against China, determined to resist such a move. One significant outcome of the Chinese–Japanese war was the reinvolvement of the United States in Asian affairs. Till late 1937, the United States maintained strict neutrality. As the American ambassador in Nanking, Nelson Johnson, stated, the United States sought a 'peaceful and friendly relationship' with both Japan and China. But because this meant that trade continued between Japan and the United States, the United States was in a sense providing part of Japan's arms being used against China. The Chinese, therefore, were highly critical of American policy, believing that trucks, cotton, iron and steel, and petroleum shipped from the United States were being used by Japanese forces against them. The *Hankow Takungpao*, an influential newspaper, denounced American neutrality, saying that the Chinese were fighting the Japanese in order to defend American interests but that they were being betrayed by Americans. The Japanese, on their part, welcomed US passivity and believed that it should be possible to bring the Chinese government to its knees if foreign intervention could be avoided.

Within just a couple of years, however, the situation reversed itself. Shedding its neutralist stand, the United States began actively intervening in East Asian affairs, providing China with political and economic assistance, while at the same time adopting punitive measures against Japan. As a result, the United States emerged as the main obstacle in the way of Japanese ambitions. Within China, both Nationalists and Communists welcomed the new American initiative, and there grew the perception that China and the United States, with the possible addition of the Soviet Union, were developing a common front against Japanese aggression. In response, the feeling of isolation grew in Japan, and this propelled the leaders to seek the way out by establishing a new order in the whole East Asian region, including the European colonies, under its domination. The result, almost inevitably, was Japan's war not only against China and the United States but also against Britain, the Netherlands, and ultimately the Soviet Union.

The pattern of a US–China combination against Japan was not destined to last. It may be said to have emerged by 1937, but by 1947–48 antagonism between the United States and the Chinese Communists, on their way to victory in the civil war, would surface, and Japan, in contrast, would become steadily incorporated into a strategic system defined by the United States for the region. In other words, there was little inevitable about the partnership of the United States and China against Japan. Nevertheless, as far as the United States is concerned, its emergence as the strongest Asian power, in contrast to Japan's loss of that status, may be said to have originated from the late 1930s. Likewise, the eventual victory of the Chinese Communists in the civil war was intimately linked to the US involvement in the Japanese–Chinese war, which enabled the Communists to emerge as patriots and organize the Chinese masses against Japan and ultimately against the Nationalists. For all these reasons, the momentous events around 1937 were to pave the way for what would develop as the basic framework of Asian affairs for several decades after the Second World War.

Why did the US–China partnership against Japan emerge after 1937? It was in part a reflection of the overall trends in international affairs. There is no need to recount in detail the course of events in Europe, starting with Nazi Germany's November 1937 decision for the conquest of Eastern Europe, through the August 1939 non-aggression pact between Germany and the Soviet Union, and the

German invasion of Poland in September, ushering in the Second World War. By the spring of 1940 the Netherlands, Belgium, France, and other countries had fallen to German arms, and only Britain remained to continue the struggle against them. But then, in June 1941, German forces invaded Soviet territory in violation of the non-aggression pact, bringing the United States into the war indirectly in the form of extending massive aid to Britain and the Soviet Union to ensure their survival. Thus in Europe, too, Germany was fighting against a combination of Britain and the Soviet Union, with the genuine possibility that the war might come to involve the United States.

These developments in Europe had immediate repercussions in Asia, where the French and Dutch colonial regimes were visibly weakened, and, as far as the British empire was concerned, the mother country's preoccupation with Germany meant it could not strengthen adequately the defences of Singapore, Burma, Australia, New Zealand, and other members of the Commonwealth.

While these events were occurring quite independently of Japanese policy, and indeed there was little Japan could do to influence them, the nation found itself inevitably drawn into the vortex and was compelled to make certain fateful choices. East Asia, which had hitherto developed with its own momentum, was fast becoming a part of the global crisis. Of course, 'the road to the Pacific war' was essentially one which the Japanese chose to take, but they might not necessarily have done so but for these rapidly changing conditions in the world. For instance, Germany hoped to make use of Japan in destroying Britain's bases and naval forces in Southeast Asia and to prevent US intervention in the European war; a Japanese–German combination, it was believed, would keep the United States preoccupied with Asia. The strategy did not work, for by then the United States was coming to identify its security with the survival of Britain; thus it would be of vital importance to preserve the British colonies in Asia. And in order to prevent Japan from attacking them, it would make sense to keep Japanese forces tied down in China. Hence the stepped-up military and economic assistance to China, as well as embargoes imposed on shipments of strategic materials to Japan. The bulk of the US navy was kept in the Pacific as a deterrent. Thus for the first time in its history, the United States actively intervened in Asian affairs – in order to defend Great Britain. This was what the Japanese–German connection brought about. Although their alliance was meant to isolate the United States, the opposite actually happened, as the Americans came to see a clear connection between their security and the developments in Europe and Asia.

United States policy and Japanese diplomacy were on a collision course, not just in China but also in Southeast Asia. In part this was an inevitable consequence of Japan's search for a self-sufficient empire; even with the conquest of Manchuria and Inner Mongolia, Japan had to continue to import large quantities of cotton, iron, petroleum, copper, and other raw materials from the United States and the European colonies in Asia. So long as self-sufficiency remained a basic national objective, this was an untenable situation, and it would be imperative to try to control the resources of Indochina, the Dutch East Indies, and their environs. That would entail military action in the South China Sea and beyond, with the result that conflict with Britain, France, the Netherlands, and the United States would become possible.

Such a strategy of southward expansion became more seriously considered after 1938, with a new impetus provided by Japanese domestic politics as well as developments in Europe. With Britain on the defensive, Japan, actively courted by Germany, soon articulated the policy for a new order in East Asia. Best exemplified by the Japanese government's declaration of 3 November, Japan was now to aim for 'the establishment of a new order for ensuring durable stability in East Asia'. That there was a domestic aspect to such a principle was evident from the assertion, in the same declaration, that 'the establishment of a new order in East Asia has its basis in the original spirit of the founding of our nation, and it is a glorious task imposed on the Japanese people today to complete it'. The pursuit of a policy towards China was now provided with a domestic context; there was to be a new order at home and abroad.

Initially, the new order comprised Japan, Manchukuo, and China; as the above-mentioned declaration stated, the 'construction of the new order aims at close cooperation among Japan, Manchukuo, and China so as to develop mutually interlinking relations among their political, economic, cultural, and other affairs'. Hirota had said more or less the same thing earlier. But now there was a greater ideological content, implying the expulsion, or at least the weakening, of Western power and influence in the region. In that sense, the new order would ultimately have to include the rest of Asia and bring about Japanese expansion into Southeast Asia.

On 18 November 1938, Foreign Minister Arita Hachirō sent a note to the American ambassador, asserting: 'Now that a new situation has arisen in East Asia, to persist in observing ideas and principles that prevailed before the incident [i.e. the war with China] will not only not help solve the problems that face us today but will not contribute to the establishment of a permanent peace in East Asia.' Here clearly was the assertion of Japan's ideological unilateralism. Ozaki Hotsumi, one of Prime Minister Konoe Fumimaro's advisers, published an essay on 'the East Asian community' for the January 1939 issue of *Chūōkōron* and provided intellectual underpinnings for the Arita note. According to Ozaki, the establishment of a new East Asian order was intended as a solution for the increasingly serious problem of nationalism in the region. Japan had the task, first of reforming itself, and then of becoming 'a liberator of Asia from its agony'. That agony was derived from the semi-colonial status and economic backwardness of Asian countries so that only the formation of an 'East Asian community', which would be a 'regional, racial, cultural, economic, and defensive combination' of Asians against 'the general world order', would free Asia from the domination of Western capitalism and point the way to new possibilities. The Asian countries, he noted, must increase their production so as to 'put an end to the status of semi-colonies and to bring about their national liberation and economic well-being'. This was the language of pan-Asianism, but one that was derived from an economic and social interpretation of history. Even the military were adopting similar language, indicating that from around 1938 the Japanese outlook on the world was becoming much more ideological than earlier.

The deepening involvement of the United States in Asian affairs can be linked to the coincidence of the developments in European affairs and the growing ideological emphasis in Japanese foreign policy. From the US perspective, the approach of war in Europe, and Japan's search for a new order in Asia, were really two sides of the same coin. They were both products of aggressive forces, and if the United States were to stop them, the task had to be carried out in Asia as well as in Europe. In order to prevent German domination of Europe, Japan's relative power would have to be weakened, and vice versa. Hence the series of steps Washington took in Asia after 1938, such as the extension of loans to China and the abrogation of the 1911 treaty of commerce with Japan. This latter step was intended to place US trade with Japan directly under governmental control so that, when occasion arose, trade embargoes could be instituted. Thus for the first time since 1931, the possibility arose that the Japanese war with China might lead to a war with the United States. Fundamentally, this was because of the American perception of the interconnectedness between events in Europe and in Asia. As Secretary of State Cordell Hull said, 'we draw the line between honest, law-abiding, peaceful countries and peoples ... on one hand, and those who are flouting law and order and officially threatening military conquest without limit as to time or extent'.

After 1939, therefore, the Japanese grew more and more concerned over their relationship with the United States, even as they were mired down in the long war in China. This situation made Southeast Asia all the more important to Japanese leaders. As US policy towards Japan hardened, they became convinced that they must expand into Southeast Asia which would have to supply oil and other materials that were in danger of being embargoed by the United States. To simplify, Japan was faced with the choice of either returning to a normal pattern of trade with the United States, which would necessitate modification of Japanese behaviour in China, or undertaking a 'southern advance', which would make a collision with the United States and Britain a real possibility. Japanese officials, put on the defensive, had to consider what sort of concessions in China would satisfy the Americans, or, barring such a compromise, whether the Americans would intervene if Japan, in the process of undertaking a southern strategy, attacked the British colonial possessions, but not US territory, in Asia.

It was unfortunate for Japan that before its leaders thoroughly discussed available alternatives and adopted a consistent strategy to cope with these urgent issues, they became once again influenced by external events. In August 1939, Germany, with which Japan was contemplating an alliance, concluded a non-aggression pact with the Soviet Union, a country which had remained a hypothetical enemy for the Japanese army. Hardly had the Japanese recovered from the shock – the prime minister resigned, saying, 'the international situation is truly beyond comprehension' – and begun groping for a sensible response to this development, than there came Germany's spring offensive of 1940. Believing that Germany would soon conquer the whole of Europe, the Japanese launched their southern strategy; they pressed the Dutch authorities in the East Indies to guarantee the continued supply of oil and rubber to Japan, placed military patrols inside the northern border of French Indochina, and demanded Britain to stop the shipment of arms to Chungking through Burma and Hong Kong. From around this time, the term 'Great East Asia' came into use, connoting not just East Asia proper but also Southeast Asia and sometimes even India. Governmental spokesmen talked of the spirit of *hakkō ichi'u* (eight corners of the world under one roof) as the principle that would be the basis for the new regional order.

Such a strategy assumed the possibility of conflict with the United States. Judging that Japan was not ready for so drastic a development, the cabinet of Admiral Yonai Miatsumasa, in office during the first half of 1940, refused to sign a formal treaty of alliance with Germany directed against the United States. But the cabinet headed by Prince Konoe Atsumaro, coming to power in July, had no such hesitation. Not that it saw a war with the United States as an immediate possibility, but it was subordinating such worries to the more immediate task of accomplishing a southern advance. Konoe and his colleagues were convinced that an alliance with Germany, which was then winning victories in Europe, would ensure that Japan would be able to expand into Southeast Asia without incurring US or British interference. A pact with Germany thus was the instrument

79

with which the Japanese sought to realize the ambition, implicit in the nation's long war in Asia, of establishing a new Asian order of economic autonomy.

At bottom was a perception of the world, originating in German geopolitics, which postulated the division of the globe into three or four blocs. Matsuoka Yōsuke, the foreign minister under Konoe, wanted to implement such a vision as the basis for ensuring Japanese security. According to him, in order to establish Japan's political and economic supremacy in Asia, the fundamental objective of national policy, it was imperative to have the powers recognize the new Asian order. A pact with Germany was the first step in this direction, which should be followed, he thought, by an understanding with the Soviet Union. As for the United States, if Japan adopted 'a resolute attitude' on the strength of these arrangements, Matsuoka believed, Washington might come to modify its policy towards Japan, thereby avoiding war between the two countries. The Axis alliance with Germany and Italy, reflecting such a strategy, explicitly stated that these two nations recognized and respected 'Japan's position of leadership in East Asia in the construction of a new order'. In return, Japan acknowledged its partners' superior position in Europe. The alliance added, in a secret clause, that if any of the three signatories were attacked by the United States, the other two would come to its assistance 'through every political, economic, and military means'.

Such a geopolitical strategy confirmed the pan-Asianist orientation of Japanese foreign policy. In a memorandum written in early 1941, Matsuoka stated that the world was to be divided into four zones: 'The Great East Asian zone, the European zone (including Africa), the American zone, and the Soviet zone (including India and Iran).' Japan was to be the 'political leader of the Great East Asian Coprosperity Sphere, with the responsibility for the maintenance of order within the area'. This would entail 'securing a superior position in the procurement of raw materials necessary for national defence' and 'governing and guiding' the colonial areas in Southeast Asia, while at the same time 'allowing as much autonomy as possible to each people according to its ability'. Highly abstract, such an idea was ideologically unambiguous and seems to have had much appeal to the

Japanese people at that time. For decades they had suffered from a sense of inferiority towards the West because of the nation's dependence on the West's resources and markets, and wondered if there might not be a fundamental conflict between East and West. Such uncomfortable thoughts could be wiped clean by adopting an aggressive agenda for the establishment of a Great East Asia under Japanese leadership that would be autonomous politically as well as economically, an East Asia in which the indigenous people would awaken to their self-identity and from which Western power and influence would be ejected.

Since the mid-nineteenth century, the Japanese had always tried to fit themselves into a Western-led diplomatic framework, geopolitically and conceptually. Now, they could at last assert something *they* postulated, the idea of a new world system consisting of regional orders, with Japan to be as autonomous in its region as the others would be in theirs. This combined national interests with a philosophy of history, concluding the search for a meaningful role in world affairs which generations of Japanese had under-taken. Not only military and civilian officials and their spokesmen, but journalists and intellectuals joined in expressing their ardent support for the vision of a new Asian order, which to many of them meant that they were finally being liberated from Western influence.

They were deluding themselves. Not only was the scheme for a Great East Asia not attainable in the real world of geopolitics, but the vision was far less Japanese, or Asian, than they thought; it was really another import from the West.

First of all, contrary to what Matsuoka and his supporters believed, the world was not neatly divided, or divisible, into four blocs. The United States refused to accept such a scheme, and Germany and the Soviet Union were about to go to war against one another. In other words, three out of the four would-be leaders of the new world order were acting contrary to Matsuoka's fond scheme. Second, the United States and the Soviet Union never abandoned their respective visions of universalism, one democratic and the other socialist, and would reject any notion that Asia stood beyond their reach. Third, as for Asians themselves, for decades the Chinese had denounced Japan's self-centred

Asianism; as early as 1934, when the Amō statement was issued, they rejected the notion that it was Japan's responsibility to maintain order in Asia; according to Chinese perception, 'Asia for Asians' simply meant 'Asia under Japanese domination' until Japan explicitly gave up its colonialism and aggression. Even though Asians were to seek their liberation from Western imperialism, the task could never be performed by Japan, an Asian imperialist, something worse than a Western imperialist.

Conceptually, the notions of new order, economic self-sufficiency, and autarky had been imported from Europe, in particular from German military science. The new East Asian order, therefore, was a Western idea. Moreover, to establish and maintain such an order through an alliance with European powers undermined the whole basis of Asianism. (Some Japanese, notably Shiratori Toshio, a Foreign Ministry official, sought to get round this logical dilemma through an absurd proposition that Germany and Italy were really less European than Asian.) Japan's totalitarian regime, too, was in part inspired by the German and Soviet examples. Thus Japan in the 1930s was intellectually and politically no less dependent on the West than earlier. To build an autonomous Asian order on such a flimsy basis was an impossible task. Nevertheless, the Japanese seem to have truly, even fanatically, believed in the vision, turning it into an obsessive ideology. Japanese diplomacy, which hitherto had sought pragmatic, specific goals in the security and economic spheres, now for the first time was driven by ideology.

Unfortunately, the viability of such an ideology, logically inconsistent as it was, hinged also on external circumstances over which Japan had little control. Only if Germany and Italy defeated Britain, only if the United States refrained from intervening in Europe and Asia, and only if Germany and the Soviet Union adhered to their non-aggression pact, would Japan have an opportunity to implement the Asian scheme. The reality, of course, was far otherwise; Britain survived the German onslaught, the United States began actively aiding Britain in Europe and in Asia, American support for China was stepped up, and Germany invaded the Soviet Union. These developments totally nullified whatever realistic basis there might have existed for the implementation of an Asianist scheme by Japan. The gap widened between the ideology and the reality, compelling the Japanese leaders to narrow the gap, either by accepting the reality or by seeking to realize the vision, no matter what the reality. They opted for the latter course. That was the meaning of 'the road to Pearl Harbor'.

The most immediate problem facing Japan in 1941, as it sought to establish the new Asian order, was policy towards the United States which was certain to stand in the way of Japan's expansion to Indochina, Singapore, the Dutch East Indies, and other parts of Southeast Asia. Without bringing the region under Japanese control, there could be no new order in East Asia, but should this be attempted even if it led to war with the United States, or should diplomatic means be utilized for the time being, to see if Japanese–US relations could somehow be ameliorated? Matsuoka and other civilian leaders persisted in the optimism that the latter option was still viable, believing that ultimately the United States would choose to recognize Japanese supremacy in Asia and avoid war with Japan. For him the signing of a neutrality treaty with the Soviet Union in April was calculated to put additional pressure on the United States to desist from intervening. In the meantime, negotiations were continued with the colonial authorities in French Indochina and the Dutch East Indies to ensure an adequate supply of petroleum and otherwise strengthen Japan's position in the region. The Japanese military, however, believed the time for diplomacy had passed and that the nation should be prepared to use force in Southeast Asia, even if this might bring about American intervention. For Japan's army and navy officers, especially section and division chiefs in the War and the Navy Departments as well as the General Staffs, 'southern expansion' and war with the United States were becoming more and more indistinguishable.

In a sense both optimists like Matsuoka and pessimists in the military were justified in their conflicting assessments of American intentions, for the Americans themselves were divided. During the first half of 1941, the Roosevelt administration did not define a consistent policy towards Japan. While the survival of Britain and its empire remained the fundamental objective, American military strategists believed they were not adequately prepared for a two-ocean war. Therefore, the United States had first to concentrate on the defence of Britain against Germany, adopting a defensive strategy in the Pacific for the time being. At the same time, however, Japan's control over Southeast Asia with its rich resources had to be prevented by all means short of war. Was there a workable strategy to produce such a result? Officials in Washington were not so sure, but they thought every possible method must be tried to gain time while the nation was getting ready for certain war in the Pacific. Thus talks were held with Japanese diplomats in Washington intermittently, military assistance for China was stepped up to tie Japanese forces down on the continent, and the bulk of the US fleet was retained in Pearl Harbor. The fact that during the spring of 1941 the Japanese themselves hesitated to use force in Southeast Asia made it possible for the United States to postpone adopting a definitive strategy.

Such uncertainty, both in Japan and the United States, came to an end after 22 June, when Germany violated the non-aggression pact and attacked the Soviet Union. This might have caused the Japanese leadership to reconsider its Asian scheme, but it decided to go ahead with its implementation, taking the fateful step of occupying the whole of Indochina in the wake of the German invasion of Soviet territory. The United States immediately retaliated, freezing Japanese assets and imposing a *de facto* embargo on shipments of petroleum to Japan. Finally, the nature of the Japan–US confrontation became clarified. Japan would seek to establish an autarkic sphere in Asia. The United States would respond by cutting off all trade with Japan. It would refuse to let Japan carry out its regional scheme. Suddenly, Japan found itself deprived of American resources *and* possibly of Southeast Asian resources unless it was willing to go to war to prevent US intervention in the region. A war with the United States thus became perceived as a part of the Asian project. The East Asian Coprosperity Sphere had to be established at all costs, and, conversely, the establishment of such a sphere was essential if Japan were to fight a war with a far more richly endowed nation like the United States. If war was inevitable, the best strategy was to strike first, to strike a blow against the US navy in the Pacific.

This was the conclusion the Japanese military had arrived at in the second half of 1941.

On 30 August, the military adopted a 'guideline for executing our national policy', which clearly stated: 'We have resolved not to hesitate to go to war against the United States (and Britain and the Dutch East Indies) in order to complete our system of autonomy and defence. We shall complete our war preparation by the end of October.' As revealed here, Japan would simultaneously attack the colonial areas in Southeast Asia and go to war against the imperial powers, including the United States. According to a General Staff document that accompanied the above guideline, 'The policy of the United States towards Japan is based on a world view that sustains the status quo and aims at world conquest and the protection of democracy. All these objectives stand in the way of our growth and expansion in East Asia.' The two nations, the paper continued, had 'diametrically opposite policies, and it is a matter of historical inevitability that their collision ... will ultimately end in war'.

Despite the determination to prepare for war to start in late October, it was actually a month afterwards that a final decision was made to attack US and British possessions in Asia and the Pacific. This was because some last-minute efforts were made to avoid such a war. It must be noted that only a small number of military leaders were convinced that Japan should never fight such a war because there was no chance to attain victory. These included Admiral Yamamoto Isoroku who remained convinced to the very end, even as he devised and directed the attack on the US fleet in Hawaii, that military collision with the United States should be avoided at all costs. The majority of those who advocated a *rapprochement* between the two countries were indulging in wishful thinking that a diplomatic solution to the Pacific crisis should be possible on the basis of a compromise, whereby the United States would agree to resume trade with Japan, while Japan in turn would desist from a forceful occupation of Southeast Asia. Such a compromise would still enable the nation to obtain the resources it needed. Even the above 'guideline' noted that if the United States and Britain agreed 'to restore trade with us and support our efforts to seek economic cooperation with Thailand and the

Dutch East Indies', Japan should be prepared to promise 'not to use our bases in Indochina for expanding by force elsewhere in Asia, except China'. In other words, the United States could avoid war by agreeing to restore normal trade relations with Japan, leaving Japan's position in China intact for the time being.

Since this option would still leave Japan in control of China, the Chinese were adamantly opposed to any such compromise. While American officials contemplated a temporary deal with Japan in order to focus on the European theatre of war, the Chinese in Chungking, and their representatives in Washington and London condemned such a step – in effect exchanging trade with Japan for the latter's pledge not to invade Southeast Asia – as totally ignoring Chinese interests and intentions. Indeed, the Japanese hoped that a compromise with the United States on Southeast Asia would lead to diminished US involvement in China. Precisely for this reason, the Americans in the end decided not to seek a settlement that would amount to obtaining Japan's agreement not to expand into Southeast Asia at the expense of China. Moreover, officials in Washington realized that so long as Japanese forces remained in China, there was no assurance that they might not again seek to expand southwards. To put an end to Japan's aggressive policy, it would be necessary not only to stop its forces from invading Southeast Asia but also to eject them from China. There could be no peace in Asia, nor security for the United States and Britain, until Japan put an end to its ten-year-long aggression and become a peace-oriented nation. Thus convinced, President Roosevelt and his advisers rejected a *modus vivendi* with Japan. The road to compromise was closed. Japan responded by going to war.

The imperial rescript of 8 December 1941, declaring war on the United States and Great Britain, is an important document detailing the factors which the Japanese leaders believed justified their decision for war. The United States and Britain, it said, had supported the Chungking regime, 'thereby prolonging the chaos in East Asia', sought to isolate Japan in collusion with other countries, 'placed every obstacle in the way of our peaceful commerce, finally adopting an economic boycott and threatening our very existence'. Japan, therefore, had to rise to the challenge 'for its existence and defence'. It is clear that the document summed up Japanese thinking, civilian as well as military, that had produced a certain self-image. Here was the image of a self-sufficient nation, an autarkic national-defence state, buttressed by the ideology of Japan's pan-Asianist mission. The imperial rescript reflected a sense of shock that this mission had been misunderstood by the powers which had instead sought to isolate and punish Japan. The Japanese had developed numerous self-images since the early Meiji years: a nation with inadequate space and resources, a nation that nevertheless wanted to modernize itself, a nation suffering from the prejudice of Western countries, a nation that would emerge as the leader of Asia. The ideology of the Great East Asian Coprosperity Sphere was a culminating point of all such ideas. The Japanese would go to war against the United States, Britain, and ultimately the whole world in the name of that ideology. That was how they had come to define their own 'existence and defence'.

Chapter 8

THE CONSEQUENCES OF THE PACIFIC WAR

From the beginning, Japan's leaders recognized that to go to war against both the United States and Great Britain was almost a suicidal act, but even they did not anticipate how quickly US forces would re-establish their power in the Pacific. On the eve of Pearl Harbor, Japanese naval and air strength in the Pacific had exceeded that of the United States, and it was hoped that, with the bulk of the US fleet having been destroyed, this supremacy would be maintained for the time being. Moreover, the Japanese believed that US military forces would have to be diverted to Europe to prevent the collapse of the Soviet Union and Britain. If, therefore, Japan could combine its force with those of Germany and the areas occupied by the two powers, there would be sufficient strength to match the enemy's military capabilities.

In reality, however, US forces in the Pacific recovered much more rapidly than expected. Between 1942 and 1943, for instance, whereas Japan produced new weapons totalling about $5 billion, the United States turned out $38 billion, a significant portion of which consisted of submarines and fighter planes for use in the Pacific theatre of the war. These proved effective in destroying Japanese battleships and aircraft-carriers, starting with the battle of Midway in June 1942. United States forces next utilized a large number of landing-craft to recapture Japanese bases in the south Pacific. In the battle of Guadalcanal, which lasted for several months between late 1942 and early 1943, Japanese forces suffered a casualty rate of 64 per cent, whereas for US forces the ratio was only 3 per cent, indicating that American military power was particularly well equipped. Furthermore, the European situation grew worse from the Japanese point of view. After 1943, as Soviet and British forces began their counter-offensive, there was little chance that Japan and Germany could combine their forces for a joint strategy.

The year 1944 marked the beginning of US bombing missions against Japanese-occupied areas in Asia and the Japanese mainland itself. The United States manufactured 96,318 fighter planes that year, in contrast to Japan's 28,180. Moreover, it is recorded that whereas only about 10 per cent of bombs used by the allies during the war were dropped on Japan, Japanese accounted for 58 per cent of the bombing victims – another indication of how vulnerable Japan was to air attack. In this sense, it was symptomatic of Japan's weakness that its decision to surrender should have been occasioned by atomic bombings by the United States. Although the Japanese army still had two million soldiers, mainly on the continent, they were of little use against US air power.

Japan's economic inferiority was also evident. The United States was the only combatant which increased its GNP during the war. As of 1944, America's national income totalled some $200 billion, double the amount for 1940. Japan's national income increased from 31 billion yen to 57 billion yen during these four years, but commodity prices doubled in the meantime, thus in fact lowering the real income of the people. Munitions production could not keep pace with their destruction, and there developed an extreme shortage of consumer goods. It may be said that Japan's economic strength, measured in terms of GNP or natural resources, was at most one-tenth of that of the United States. Likewise, whereas American women and senior citizens made up for young men sent to the front, there was a chronic shortage of labour in Japan, resulting in the compulsory shipment of workers from Korea and China to Japan. Working conditions were severe, and many workers died, especially in mines.

Japan had been mobilized since 1938 through the national mobilization law, but economic controls had not worked well, owing to bureaucratic squabbling and the lack of coordination between government and private industry. Munitions production had never achieved its goals, and it was only in the latter part of 1943 that a Munitions Ministry was established in order to centralize the production of weapons. In the United States, in contrast, the War Production Board functioned effectively and exercised leadership in promoting cooperation between management and business, and between industry and the armed forces. Aeroplanes, ships, tanks, and other items were manufactured in accordance with planning. The result was that the United States produced more than a hundred times as many cars as Japan, and similar gaps existed in the production of oil, iron and steel, and other essential commodities. As US planes and submarines shut off Japan's sea lanes after 1944, and as its industrial cities were destroyed by bombing, Japan's productive capacity had been reduced to one-half of the prewar level by the time Japan surrendered. Clearly, the United States had achieved complete economic victory over Japan.

How about their ideological conflict, pitting America's universalism against Japan's particularism, or America's internationalism against Japan's pan-Asianism? Here the picture was more complex, since, unlike the military or economic realm, it is difficult to measure success quantitatively in this field. But at least it may be noted that the Axis powers were never able to produce anything resembling the United Nations' declaration, signed by the United States and its forty-odd allies in January 1942, endorsing the 'four freedoms' and other aspects of the Atlantic charter (August 1941). Japan, to be sure, sought to counter American universalism through enunciating a particularistic doctrine of pan-Asian regionalism. But it never received the support of the bulk of Asian people. A few of them, such as Wang Ching-wei of China and Chandra Bose of India, did believe that a new Asian order under Japanese leadership would lead to Asian liberation from Western imperialism, but they were never able to lead the national-liberation movements of the colonial areas but instead were denounced as puppets of Japanese imperialism.

Nationalism in Asia had become a notable force before the war in India, China, Indonesia, Indochina, and elsewhere, and there is little doubt that Japan's initial successes in the war caused Western prestige to plummet, thereby strengthening the nationalistic sentiment throughout the region. But Asian nationalism had been inspired less by Japan's pan-Asianism than by the Wilsonian principle of self-determination and by the Soviet-initiated anti-imperialism. In China, where pan-Asianism and allied ideology vied for influence, neither the Kuomintang nor the Communists accepted Japanese ideology, but instead continued to be influenced by American and Soviet ideas. Even someone like Chiang Kai-shek, who preferred traditional Chinese thought to modern Western ideology, never considered a spiritual union with Japan and repeatedly denounced the Great East Asian Coprosperity Sphere concept as hypocritical. *Takungpao*, one of China's major dailies, asserted that the idea of a Japan-led Asia was nothing but 'a conspiracy to deceive the allies', and that a real peace for Asia would come only after Japanese ambitions had been defeated. In short, compared with American-style universalism, Japan's pan-Asianism had little appeal even to Asians, much less to other people in the world. The victory of the United States in the war of ideas was clearly demonstrated at the San Francisco conference in the spring of 1945 which resulted in the establishment of a new United Nations organization whose charter incorporated the ideas of the Atlantic charter.

In fact, by then the Japanese themselves were accepting some of the American-inspired ideas. The idea of Asia for Asians which had existed for some time began subtly changing itself to embrace the idea of an Asia that accepted universalistic principles, or an Asia where these principles were better practised than elsewhere. For instance, the Great East Asia conference held in Tokyo in November 1943 adopted a declaration calling on the Asian countries 'to develop friendly ties with all nations, abolish racial barriers, engage in cultural exchange, open up natural resources, and thereby contribute to the world's development'. Such principles were little different from those enunciated in the Atlantic charter. It is, of course, difficult to say to what extent these ideas had come to be embraced by Japanese leaders. Nor can it be said that such universalistic language was now replacing the anti-Western pan-Asianism that they had been enunciating. But the very fact that some Japanese were trying to universalize even their pan-Asianism – in other words, saying that Americans and Japanese pursued identical objectives but that Asian areas under Japan were truer to these principles than areas under American influence – indicated America's success in winning the ideological battle. For to apply universalistic values to Asia was tantamount to undermining the ideological foundation of the Great East Asian Coprosperity Sphere.

Nevertheless, pan-Asianist doctrine never disappeared till the end. That was because Japan's leaders persisted in believing that the Pacific war held some meaning, that it was not a war of aggression fought for self-interest or territorial expansion. Even if they were to be defeated, they wanted to believe that the war had been fought for the liberation of Asia. As Shigemitsu Mamoru, wartime foreign minister, wrote after the war, 'as soon as the objectives for which we were fighting the war could be achieved, peace could be restored at any moment'. War objectives he had in mind were precisely those enunciated in the declaration of the Great East Asian conference, such as freedom and economic development for Asian countries. These were virtually identical with US war aims. Therefore, even if the nation were to lose the war, it would be possible to say that the war aims had been, at least partially if not totally, achieved. At least that was how Japan's leaders persuaded themselves as they surrendered; they told them- selves that they had won the war even while losing the battle.

Thus, subjectively speaking, the Japanese could argue that Japan's defeat did not mean an ideological failure. They had been no match to the United States in military or economic strength, but nothing had been wrong with their ideas or ideals. The development of postwar Asian nationalism, and the independence of many Asian countries, would come to be seen by Japan's pan-Asianists as a vindication of their faith. In reality, of course, Asian liberation owed much less to pan-Asianist doctrine than to the universalism of the United States. Therefore, it would be more correct to say that in ideology, too, the United States was the victor. Still, it is doubtful if this fact was realized by the Japanese. Fifty years after the defeat, they are still divided about the meaning of the Pacific war. Unlike the Germans, they have not unanimously, or totally, rejected the ideological basis of the war they fought.

The collapse of the Japanese empire in August 1945 also meant the collapse of an international order in which Japan as a great power had played a role. The post-1945 world was one that was defined fundamentally by the military supremacy of the two superpowers, the United States and the Soviet Union. Of course, to the extent that a balance between them was critical to the international order, the situation was little different from the pre-1940 pattern of international relations in which a plurality of powers had maintained (or threatened to destroy) some sort of equilibrium. But the bipolar power balance this time was characterized by a number of new factors. First, in addition to some tacit understanding about their respective spheres of influence – something the allies had discussed at their wartime conferences – the superpowers equipped themselves with nuclear weapons, thereby obliterating traditional boundaries defined territorially. Future wars were conceptualized as air wars which might begin unexpectedly with a strategic bombing of cities. Both sides were already beginning their plans for a third world war.

Nevertheless, some sort of balance between the two superpowers was maintained for a while after the war. Sometimes referred to as the Yalta system – after the Yalta meeting of Roosevelt, Churchill and Stalin in February 1945 – this balance was based on the understanding that the Soviet Union would enjoy positions of special influence in Eastern Europe, the Baltic, and northeast Asia, while the United States would retain its superior power in the Western hemisphere and most of the Pacific. There were, to be sure, grey areas not included in either sphere of influence, such as the Middle East and China, but there was no US – USSR military confrontation in these places. Moreover, although both undertook nuclear armament, they were not yet engaging in an arms race. Before 1950, the defence budgets of the United States averaged about $13 billion a year, hardly 5 per cent of the GNP. The US armed forces in 1947 were only about a tenth of what they had been at the end of the war. Soviet defence spending was roughly the same, which suggests that, given the far smaller size of the Soviet economy, the production of consumer goods had to be sacrificed. Even so, this was hardly a situation of military confrontation by the two powers.

Why, then, did their relations come to be known as 'the Cold War'? This suggests the importance of ideology in postwar international relations. It may have been an inevitable consequence of a war that had stressed the role of ideas. Since the allies' victory was seen as a victory of their ideas over the Axis ideologies, it was naturally expected that the same ideas would form the basis of postwar international affairs. Events after the war, however, belied such expectations. Soviet support for communist parties in Eastern Europe, or US aid to the Nationalists in the Chinese civil war, soon generated the impression that the super-powers had little in common ideologically. Already by 1946, it became commonplace to contrast American liberalism, capitalism, and democracy to Soviet communism and totalitarianism. It was as if the world were becoming divided into the liberal and the socialist camps. Such an image was a gross over-simplification of international relations; the world was never really split into two ideological camps. Still, the dichotomy had enormous influence and came to affect profoundly the public opinion and domestic politics of many countries. This was an interesting phenomenon, suggesting that ideology was playing an even more crucial role than military factors in defining international affairs at that time.

There was also an economic dimension to the picture. Here the United States enjoyed undisputed supremacy. Its GNP amounted to $211.9 billion in 1945, or about one-half of the total wealth of the world. The situation continued for several years after the war, resulting in America's perpetual export surplus; as its industrial and agricultural products were shipped overseas, other countries were recording trade deficits *vis-à-vis* the United States, complicating the task of reconstruction. Not surprisingly, the United States had to provide them with much economic aid, the most important of which was the Marshall Plan, contributing billions of dollars of assistance to Western European countries.

America's economic hegemony was also behind the establishment of the Bretton Woods system, including the International Monetary Fund and the International Bank for Reconstruction and Development (commonly known as the World Bank). American funds provided much of the initial resources for these organizations. Even more important, the dollar now functioned as the international medium of exchange. Its value was fixed in terms of gold (i.e. one ounce of gold was set at $35.00), and other currencies would be converted into dollars at fixed rates of exchange. Trade and other transactions were carried out in the US currency, and each country's dollar holdings ('exchange reserve') could be sold for gold at the same price. It was in the 1950s that this system was implemented, but even before then, it was clear that international economic transactions hinged on the strength of the US economy and its currency. With such strength, the United States set about developing an economically interdependent international order. The Marshall Plan for European recovery was but the first step.

If international relations at that time had been defined primarily in economic terms, as had been the case during the 1920s, there might have been no US–Soviet confrontation, for there really was no match between the two powers in the economic sphere. The fact that the Cold War developed suggests that economics took a back seat to ideology. The American people were fully aware of their economic supremacy, but they were also afraid of the spread of Soviet ideology. A peculiar psychology of that time led them to be fearful of Russian ideas rather than confident of their economic strength. But this phenomenon was not limited to the United States. The Soviet Union and other countries, too, demonstrated a Cold War mentality as they groped for the creation of postwar international order. The costs were to prove enormous.

Japan in defeat played no role in the unfolding drama of postwar international affairs, but this did not prevent the nation from becoming involved in them. Militarily, for instance, Japanese demilitarization created new problems for regional order. At the time of surrender, there were two million Japanese forces on the Asian continent, and another million elsewhere in the Pacific. Now they were all disarmed and sent home. A few, to be sure, stayed in Burma, Indonesia, and elswhere to join anti-colonial struggles, or remained in China to fight in the civil war between the Nationalists and the Communists. That did not alter the fact, however, that the Imperial Japanese army and navy had ceased to exist. Their officers were arrested and interned, many of them to wait trial and possible execution. Military matériel, ships, and aircraft were confiscated and disposed of as the victors saw fit. Such organizations of the war machine as the Imperial Headquarters and the General Staffs of the army and navy were demolished. In terms of actual military power, Japan was back where it had been at the end of the Tokugawa period in the 1860s, indeed even before that.

In the international arena, Japan's defeat meant the disappearance of a huge empire whose power had extended over Korea, Taiwan, South Sakhalin, the Kuriles, Manchuria and most of China, and Southeast Asia. Although it was far from certain what would replace such power and how a new regional order would be defined, at least it was obvious that in a world being shaped by the military power of the United States and the Soviet Union, Japan's position would be a vastly reduced one. Such a status was confirmed through Japanese demilitarization, something that was turned into a principle of the new Japan in the constitution adopted in 1946. Its preamble and article nine, however conflicting interpretations people read (and have read) into them, clearly announced that Japan would never again become a military power. But this was only part of the emerging Asian order. Equally crucial was the presence of US power in Japan and elsewhere in Asia. At first, it was believed that US forces would be kept in Japan to ensure Japan's demilitarization and to prevent its rearmament, but by 1947, some, like General Douglas MacArthur, supreme commander of the allied powers occupying Japan, were saying that Japan's disarmament had been accomplished, thereby ending the most important mission of the US occupation forces. Indeed, MacArthur himself began advocating an early end to the occupation and the conclusion of a peace treaty with the former enemy.

Had such steps been taken in 1947, the subsequent history of US–Japan relations or of Japanese foreign affairs would have taken a very different shape. While the Yalta formula, presupposing US predominance in the western Pacific, including Japan, might have remained essentially intact, there might have developed powerful forces to push Japan to permanent demilitarization and even neutrality. Or else, the Cold War tensions between the superpowers might have led to serious ideological and political divisions in Japan, inviting US or Soviet intervention. In reality, of course, these developments did not take place because US forces remained in the country even after its disarmament had been completed. A US–Japan peace treaty would not be concluded for several more years. A key factor which produced these developments was disagreement among American officials about the duration and scale of the US military presence in Japan. In contrast to MacArthur, many, especially in the newly established Defence Department, argued that the occupation of Japan should be continued for a while longer in order to preserve US military strength in the western Pacific. They were particularly alarmed over the civil war in China, as Communist power steadily extended itself. Such a situation would inevitably affect the regional balance of power. While few American officials advocated military intervention in the Chinese civil war, many were concerned that, should China fall under the Communists, *and* if Japan remained disarmed, it would become extremely difficult to maintain a stable regional order in Asia and the Pacific. For these reasons, they argued that it would be necessary to continue the occupation of Japan and not to consider concluding a peace treaty in the near future. Between MacArthur's and the Pentagon's positions, various other alternatives were discussed in Washington, but it was not till late 1949 that a systematic review of policy towards Japan was undertaken.

In the meantime, in Japan, too, serious discussion began to be held regarding its military position. The new constitution, of course, had to be observed, and public opinion was overwhelmingly in favour of Japanese demilitarization. But at the same time, officials and opinion leaders wondered how the nation could defend itself when it remained unarmed. Already in July 1947, Foreign Minister Ashida Hitoshi was coming to the view that it would be desirable to keep US troops in Japan even after a peace treaty had been signed. If that proved impossible to arrange, then Ashida was willing to countenance some programme of Japanese rearmament within the limits set by the constitution. At this time, however, his was a lone voice, for neither Japan nor the United States had come to a decision regarding the future of Japanese security policy.

It was perhaps in the economic sphere, rather than in military policy, that the United States developed a clearer perspective. Japanese leaders cooperated with Americans in developing, by 1948, a blueprint for the nation's economic recovery and eventual reintegration into the world economy. It is estimated that Japan's national income at the time of surrender was about 360 billion yen. What this meant in dollar terms is difficult to say, as the rate of exchange changed drastically; a dollar was worth two yen through the 1930s, about four yen on the eve of Pearl Harbor, and about 270 yen by 1946–47. In 1949 the official rate of 360 yen to a dollar was established. If we use the 1946–47 rate of exchange, Japan's national income in 1946 was only about $1.3 billion, or less than one-fifth of the 1941 figure. Japan's per capita income had fallen from about $100 to $13 in the same period. This decline, of course, reflected the destruction of industry brought about by bombing raids, the steady erosion of the civilian economy during the long period of war, the virtual disappearance of foreign trade, and other factors. Particularly serious was the drastic food shortage after the war. The loss of overseas colonies meant Japan had lost important sources of rice and other necessities. Their shrinking volume had to be shared by an increasing population, as millions of Japanese soldiers and colonizers returned home. There inevitably resulted a serious inflation of commodity prices.

Postwar Japanese leaders, confronting such a dire situation, shared the conviction that for such a country, the only salvation lay in foreign trade. These leaders, to be sure, were not the same individuals as those who had dominated the scene before 1945. Some 200,000 militarists, politicians, businessmen, and others were purged from official positions, if they were not tried as war criminals. The new leaders were either younger officials in the bureaucracies – the bureaucratic structure itself was not demolished by the occupation authorities – or older men (such as Shidehara Kijūrō and Yoshida Shigeru) who had been ostracized in the 1930s and during the war as pro-British or pro-American and removed from positions of influence. These new leaders quickly organized political parties as well as study groups to plan for the nation's economic recovery. As they saw the situation, trade was going to be if anything even more crucial than before the war. Prior to 1940 Japanese trade had been more or less evenly divided between Western nations (in particular the United States) and Asian countries (mostly Japanese colonies and spheres of influence). Both these avenues now appeared lost, but without the resumption of foreign trade, there was no way the people could be fed or provided with consumer goods as well as raw materials. But to pay for these imports, it would be imperative to export manufactured goods. If, somehow, foreign trade could be resumed, it would necessitate domestic industrialization, which might lead to improved living conditions and ultimately to economic recovery.

Some such ideas became an article of faith for Japan's postwar leaders. But whether Japan would be allowed to resume trade activities would depend on the international environment, especially the existence of a global economic system that would accept a trading Japan. Interestingly enough, Japanese officials appear to have entertained some hope in this regard. In September 1946, for instance, the research bureau of the Foreign Ministry reported that 'the world economy, under the leadership of the United States, appears to be moving in the direction of doing away with autarkies and other obstacles to trade and promoting international commerce to the fullest extent'. Prewar Japan, of course, had established an autarkic system, but that had been demolished. If, after the war, other autarkies, too, could be abolished, to be replaced by an open international economic system, Japan clearly stood to benefit.

Of course, even if such a system was established, Japan would have to be admitted into it. Fortunately for the nation, the occupation authorities, with the support of officials in Washington, permitted it to resume trade as early as August 1947. Instead of the initial emphasis on instituting a variety of economic controls over Japan, such as the dissolution of *zaibatsu* (business combinations), agricultural reform, and reparations, the United States government was coming to the view that Japan's economic recovery should be effected through industrialization and trade. It was believed that Asia's economic development would also be promoted through the region's trade relations with Japan. This shift, which was a fortunate circumstance for Japan, is often characterized as a 'reverse course' in occupation policy, reflecting the intensifying Cold War between the superpowers. However, as far as economic policy towards Japan was concerned, there really was no radical reversal. For, during the Pacific war, American leaders had insisted that the postwar international order must be an open and multilateral one, and they had assumed that such an order would have to integrate a defeated Japan in order to ensure its peaceful behaviour. After all, one of the 'four freedoms' which had constituted America's war aims had been 'freedom from want', and an interdependent world economy was considered of critical importance in realizing the goal. In such a perspective, the encouragement of Japanese economic recovery after 1947 was a direct continuity of wartime thinking. It was the harsh measures of 1945–47 that were the exception. Even these measures, moreover, were designed to demilitarize and democratize the Japanese economy, goals that would necessitate the imposition of restrictions on the armament industry and the removal of agricultural and industrial concentrations. These objectives could now be said to have been largely achieved.

In any event, between 1947 and 1949 US economic policies towards Japan were in general accord with what the Japanese leaders wanted. During this brief period not only was Japanese trade resumed, but the small-scale shipments of reparations goods to other Asian countries which had been going on were terminated. The manufacturing of iron, steel, and other goods necessary for trade was started up again, and the rate of exchange was set at 360 yen to the dollar. This was perhaps an underestimation of the value of the Japanese currency, but it certainly helped to expand Japan's export trade rapidly. Starting from a virtual zero at the end of the war, it reached 174 million dollars by 1947, 258 million dollars in 1948, and 510 million dollars in 1949. Imports for these years amounted to 524 million, 684 milli on, and 905 million dollars, respectively. Thus, there were huge trade deficits, reflecting Japan's importation of large quantities of foodstuffs and raw materials (especially cotton), the bulk of which came from the United States. To pay for these purchases, Japan had to rely upon US assistance, especially through GARIOA (Government Appropriation for Relief in Occupied Areas) funding. But such largesse could not be expected to continue for ever, and the Japanese recognized the supreme importance of expanding their export trade. Here Asian countries would be of particular importance. In 1947, China's share in Japanese trade was about 3 per cent and the share of India and Pakistan combined came to about the same proportion. This was, to be sure, a steep decline from the prewar figures. Before the war, China alone had accounted for about 30 per cent of total Japanese trade. Now Japan was much more dependent on the American trade. Moreover, the civil war in China impeded the growth of trade between the two countries. Nevertheless, it is significant that there was as much as one million dollars worth of trade between China and Japan, suggesting the possibility that once the civil war ended the trade would grow faster. At that time, both American and Japanese officials assumed that even if China should come under Communist rule, that would not prevent trade relations from developing. In other words, quite apart from geopolitical considerations or ideological differences, economic internationalism was developing with its own momentum.

At the same time, it must also be noted that there was an important ideological component to US–Japanese relations at that time. If, as seen above, the Cold War was as much an ideological as a geopolitical phenomenon, it had obvious implications for Japan. Americans would come to view Japan more favourably than China, and the Japanese, in their turn, would come to consider it desirable to be closer to the United States than to China. In other words, a complete reversal of the wartime pattern of US–Japan–China relations was taking place.

At bottom was the general agreement in official American circles that Japan was to be reformed through democratization. Even during the war, State Department officials had believed that there were 'a large number of moderates or liberals in Japan, through whom it should be possible to undertake political reform and to promote liberalism'. Of course, there was no consensus as to what specifically was meant by political reform or liberalism. Americans were divided, for instance, on whether conservatives such as the emperor and his court circles were to be viewed as agents for reform in postwar Japan, or whether labour union leaders, socialists, and others who had hitherto been excluded from seats of power should be actively supported to carry out democratic reforms. There was much inconsistency among the occupation personnel concerning such issues. Nevertheless, at least insofar as postwar Japan's external affairs were concerned, there was more unity than diversity in American views. All officials believed that Japan should be rid of its pan-Asianist philosophy and instead encouraged to develop universalistic, internationalist tendencies. In order to bring about such reorientation in Japanese thought, the occupation regime undertook educational reforms, rewrote history and geography textbooks, introduced a new school system, and sought to eradicate excessive nationalism and pan-Asianism through purges and censorship. Scholars and journalists who had been active on behalf of nationalistic or pan-Asianist doctrine were prohibited from publishing anything. They would be replaced by liberals and radicals.

There is little doubt that such measures amounted to the Americanizing of Japanese thought. But there was the strong faith among Americans that what was 'American' was far more universalistic than what was considered 'Japanese' or 'Asian', and could constitute a more plausible foundation of a peaceful international order. The faith in the four freedoms remained strong, and it was firmly believed that the freedom of religion and the freedom of thought were particularly crucial in building a new world order. Reforms in Japan, therefore, although they were being imposed from above, and although these freedoms did not really exist in occupied Japan, could be justified as necessary for preparing the country for eventual participation in the international community. The suppression of state Shinto or pan-Asianism would, it was thought, ensure the growth of a healthy internationalism in Japan. Only when all countries developed an internationalist mentality, Americans believed, would there emerge a peaceful world. The preamble to the United Nations charter, or its 1948 'universal declaration of human rights', exemplified such a mentality. While promulgating these ideals, Americans believed they were speaking for the shared aspirations of mankind.

Unfortunately, by 1949 it was becoming evident that the allegedly universalistic principles embodied in these documents were not really being shared by the Soviet Union and other socialist states. These nations instead accused the United States of trying to impose its own ideology on the rest of the world. Instead of an ideologically uniform world order, international affairs became characterized by the ideological rift of the Cold War. For Japan this meant that, even as it was being prepared for incorporation into a new world order defined by the United States (and by the United Nations charter), it was also becoming identified with one side in the ideological divide.

It cannot be said, however, that the Japanese were merely passive witnesses to their own drama. For, rather than blindly following the US lead or being forced to accept American ideas, they discussed these questions quite seriously and were aware that they had a choice from a variety of definitions of world affairs. For instance, there was much discussion of how best to construct 'a nation of culture', that is, to reconstruct the nation through cultural efforts after its reliance on military power had ended in disaster. The preoccupation with cultural issues reflected the realization that Japan's militarism and pan-Asianism had revealed a poverty of ideas, and therefore that if Japan were to start afresh as a peaceful nation its culture and ideology must be transformed. In the April 1947 issue of *Sekai*, Abe Tomoji, a philosopher and literary critic, stated, 'people are saying that Japanese culture must be connected to the world's culture. This means that we must be self-conscious about the relationship between past and present and ascertain to ourselves who we really are.' The cultural crisis facing the nation was so serious as to compel the Japanese to ask 'who they really are'. As another author pointed out in the same magazine: 'As the long-standing feudal foundations of our country have crumbled, Japanese culture which has blossomed as a product of such a tradition is being severely criticized.' Similarly, a writer noted, 'It is much easier to find good and appropriate books knowledgeable about the West, but virtually zero when it comes to useful writings about the East.' All such expressions marked the loss of confidence of Japanese intellectuals who had so strongly asserted their identity as Asians.

Prince Higashikuni, the first postwar prime minister, called on the Japanese people to realize that 'We cannot live alone. We must find ways to live in prosperity with other people by making a contribution to the development of world culture on the basis of coexistence and coprosperity.' It was important 'to devote all our intellect, and all our abilities, to the development of human civilization and to the progress of mankind'. Education Minister Maeda Tamon agreed, remarking: 'For the new age, there is only one path open to Japan. Instead of arms, we must choose culture. Through our education and true morality, we must contribute to the world's progress.' At a Diet session of 5 September 1945, a representative, Tōgō Minoru, was already speaking of the need to create a 'Japan that embodied culture, economics, and peace'.

Such an idea, that postwar Japan must link itself to the rest of the world, not through arms but through cultural and economic relations, seems to have been widely shared at that time. But it would be wrong to say that it was an idea forced upon the Japanese by the occupation authorities. Rather, it may be argued that an undercurrent of cultural thought that had been suppressed in an earlier, more nationalistic and pan-Asianist climate was being unleashed in the new international environment. For, at bottom, the culturalism of postwar Japan assumed that the Japanese people's salvation lay in becoming 'global citizens' (as the newspaper, *Asahi*, noted), parting with a narrow nationalism or pan-Asianism. The path of universalism, rather than particularism, or of internationalism rather than nationalism, provided the ideological starting point for postwar Japanese foreign policy.

This universalism, the idea that Japan must link its existence to the larger world community, may be termed the new internationalism. It expressed the hope that the nation could make a contribution to the well-being of humankind through cultural exchanges and cooperative programmes undertaken with other countries. While this ideal was to be maintained for decades, its specific implementation also gave rise to serious debate among Japanese. The principles of universalism and internationalism, for instance, might have called for Japan engaging in extensive exchanges not only with the West but also with the Soviet Union and other communist countries and their political parties so as to promote world peace and mutual understanding. In reality, however, the Soviet-bloc nations had their own ideological systems that rejected Western liberalism and democratic thought. In such a situation, it was no easy task to define what Japan should do to promote internationalism. Some argued that Japan should cooperate with all countries, including the Soviet Union and Communist China. In their view, Japan should not ally itself with one side in the Cold War but should try to mediate between the two to explore possibilities for peaceful coexistence. Such views later developed into a call for a peace treaty with all former enemies, not just with the United States and its Cold War allies. On the other hand, those under Marxist and radical influences took an explicitly pro-Soviet stance. They were particularly impressed with the anti-war stand of the Japanese Communist party during the war and insisted on further reform programmes in postwar Japan as well as a more vigorous prosecution of war criminals. They criticized the apparent changes in the US occupation policy after 1947 and, for the same reason, opposed a peace treaty with only one side in the Cold War.

There were, however, those who were avowedly pro-US and anti-Soviet. Yoshida Shigeru, who served as prime minister for many years after 1948, was the most prominent of this group, but there were many others, including the so-called 'old liberals' as well as anti-Communists. They believed that Japan had always been ideologically close to the United States and Britain. The nation had nevertheless gone to war against these countries 'as a temporary aberration', as Yoshida said. Japan during the war had not been its true self, and now that the war had ended in a disaster, it should never again make the same mistake but choose to cooperate with the Western democracies. This was all the more the case since freedom, human dignity, individualism, democracy, and other universalistic values were being suppressed in the Soviet-bloc countries.

It may be said that this type of pro-Western view reflected the Americanization of postwar Japanese culture. For even the idea of 'Japan as a nation of culture' was coming to mean a Japan that was culturally Americanized. There was overwhelming American influence in Japanese education, scholarship, and entertainment, and even 'freedom' as understood by the Japanese was little more than what they took to be American freedom, something they learned from American films and magazines. Because such 'culture' was truly liberating, most Japanese felt they were right in choosing the United States as a model over the Soviet Union or Communist China with their emphasis on economic equality, social justice, class struggle, or proletarian dictatorship.

There was, however, a fourth option that was advocated by a small minority of Japanese thinkers at that time. They did not support the wholesale embrace of American culture, or of communism or Marxism, but instead insisted that Japan should identify itself with Asian nationalism, including the Chinese variety. Theirs was a more Asian-oriented universalism than the perspectives presented by the pro-American groups, believing that Japan should find its salvation in the non-Western part of the world, not in Western values. As Takeuchi Yoshimi, perhaps the best example of this group of thinkers, argued, Japan's disastrous war and defeat showed the bankruptcy of the policy of superficial Westernization; the nation should now turn to China for inspiration, for that country had succeeded in modernizing itself even while rejecting Westernization. This type of thinking had something in common with prewar pan-Asianism, except that the emphasis now was on Japan's need to learn from China and from Asia, not the other way round.

Indeed, nationalism in non-Western parts of the globe was evidently emerging as a major factor in international relations even then, and one may even argue that nationalism was to prove the most important ideology in postwar world affairs, even more important than either liberalism or communism. In the early postwar years, however, such a perspective did not command the support of most thinkers because of the inescapable presence of the Cold War ideological confrontation. Besides, during the US occupation, information on China and other Asian countries was rather meagre, and China itself was being torn apart by the civil war, making it difficult for Japanese and Chinese to interact extensively. Under the circumstances, it is not surprising that this fourth viewpoint gained relatively few adherents.

Chapter 9

THE RESUMPTION OF JAPANESE DIPLOMACY

Until about 1949, the Cold War was primarily characterized by ideological and political antagonism between the United States and the Soviet Union. But then it steadily came to take on a military character, so that by 1952, when Japan regained independence, international affairs had come to signify a world divided militarily. Put another way, the ideological confrontation was being elevated to a military level because of the failure of the two sides to contain the crisis, and because the world had neither an effective mechanism nor a strong movement to prevent such a development.

Already in 1949, the United States joined the Western European countries as well as Canada to form the North Atlantic Treaty Organization, the first peacetime alliance the nations had ever formed. It is true that at first there was much ambiguity about NATO (for instance, whether it was to entail the stationing of US forces in Europe, or whether West Germany was going to join the system), but it was clearly aimed at the Soviet Union and the Eastern bloc, thus confirming the division of Europe into two military camps. The Soviet Union, for its part, had kept its troops in Eastern European countries, and, in Asia, signed treaties of alliance with Communist China and North Korea. (Korea had become divided in 1948 into the Democratic People's Republic of Korea north of the thirty-eighth parallel and the Republic of Korea to the south.)

The militarization of such a polarized world was evident in the defence expenditures of the two super-powers. As noted above, before 1949 their military budgets had not been particularly large, but then the situation changed rather drastically. The US defence spending increased from $13.0 billion in 1949 to $33.3 billion two years later. This, of course, was due to the expenses of the Korean war, but even before its outbreak, the draft NSC-68, the document prepared by the National Security Council for coping with Cold War challenges, had called for substantial increases in defence outlays. The Soviet Union, in the meantime, successfully conducted atomic tests in 1949 and continued to augment its armed forces. Whereas its actual defence expenditure in 1950 was roughly one-half of the US figure, even this accounted for a larger share of the Soviet national income than the corresponding figure for the United States. Without doubt, starting around 1950 the superpowers were engaging themselves in an arms race.

This situation was confirmed during the Korean war. America's quick response to the North Korean invasion of the south, in June 1950, was not surprising, given the militarization of the Cold War which had already begun to take place. Thus, for the Soviet Union a successful unification of the Korean peninsula by Pyongyang would turn the Asian military balance in its favour, while, for exactly the same reason, the United States would have to prevent such an outcome. Moreover, the Americans were determined to stop Communist China's liberation of Taiwan, for such a step would also add to Soviet-bloc power.

The Cold War, in other words, was turning into a military conflict in Asia, involving not only the United States' confrontation with the Soviet Union but also with the People's Republic of China, which came to view the United States as an enemy that was trying to prevent the unification of the country. When US troops pushed beyond the thirty-eighth parallel in the Korean peninsula, Chinese forces entered the scene to face this challenge. Elsewhere in Asia, the United States supported South Vietnam (Vietnam had been ruled by two regimes, in Hanoi and Saigon, since 1949), the Philippines (which became independent in 1946), as well as Australia and New Zealand with which there was concluded a military alliance known as ANZUS. In Europe, in the meantime, the militarization of the Cold War proceeded apace, with the stationing of US forces, the participation of Greece and Turkey in NATO, and the seemingly permanent division of Germany into two halves.

The increasingly militarized Cold War also had economic and ideological dimensions. Economically, the Export Control Act, which was adopted in 1949, made up a list of goods to be embargoed from Communist-bloc nations. The embargo policy was to be binding not just on the United States but also on its allies. The Soviet side, on its part, promoted the policy of self-sufficiency so as not to have to rely upon capitalist countries for its industrialization and other economic programmes. Thus the Soviet Union offered China a loan in excess of $300 million, and the Soviet-bloc nations accounted for 70 to 80 per cent of China's trade – the remainder consisted of trade with Japan, Britain and other non-communist countries – indicating Communist China's determination to increase agricultural and industrial production without having to turn to Western capital and technology.

In ideology, too, the US–USSR confrontation became even more serious than earlier. The McCarthyism phenomenon in the United States is a good example. From the eve of the Korean war to its end, government officials, intellectuals, journalists, and even film stars who had known Soviet or Chinese Communists or who had expressed favourable opinions about them were ostracized and forced to explain or recant their positions. All this took place in a country that had fought a war in the name of freedom of expression. It was hardly surprising that in Soviet-bloc countries censorship was even more tightened than earlier.

Such a situation suggests that the Cold War was becoming a 'total war', except that it was not a real war. Just because there was no US–USSR military clash, it did not mean there was no genuine conflict. American writers noted at that time that 'the Cold War is in fact a real war', or that 'the Third World War has already begun'. Historians refer to the emergence of a 'national security state' to suggest that in such circumstances the entire country was put in a state of alert. Not just in military preparedness, but even more in domestic society, people were exhorted to be mindful that their actions and their words could benefit the enemy. It was, of course, the ultimate crime to spy for the other side, to be punished by death. Both in the United States and the Soviet Union, many trials were held to ferret out presumed agents of the other side. Under the circumstances, no third way, no ideological neutrality, seemed possible. Chinese leaders used the phrase, 'leaning to one side', in the global Cold War. The same expression could be used elsewhere to describe a situation where one had to be either for one side or the other. 'Better dead than red', a popular phrase in the United States in the 1950s, typified such an attitude.

There were individuals everywhere even then, however, who were deeply disturbed by such polarity and wondered if liberalism and capitalism on one side, and communism on the other, were the only choices facing humanity. One possible answer was a new Asianism, an idea of Asian identity separate from both the US and the Soviet camps. It will be seen in the next chapter that this movement picked up momentum only after the end of the Korean war. In the meantime, various thinkers were convinced that the only alternative to the Cold War confrontation was a peace ideology that transcended the bipolar antagonism and united, rather than dividing, humankind. Many pacifists saw no real alternative to total disarmament, even accepting the implication that in case of an external aggression a nation should desist from armed resistance. This sort of old-fashioned pacifism, however, did not become an influential movement at that time. As a result, the ideology of global polarity was allowed to remain hegemonic until a viable alternative should make its appearance.

To return to Japanese foreign affairs, the intensification of the Cold War provided the framework in which steps were taken to terminate the US occupation, to replace it with a security arrangement which may be called 'the San Francisco system', after the peace conference held in that city in 1951. By then, the Japanese economy had begun to show signs of recovery. Already by 1949 Japan's national income had reached $7.6 billion, a 40 per cent increase over the preceding year. Japan's total trade amounted to $1.3 billion, or about the level of 1941. The Japanese recovery was in sharp contrast to China's economic disarray due to the civil war; by 1949, the volume of total Japanese trade exceeded China's.

From around that time, the US government began reformulating its policy towards Japan. In view of the Communist victory in the Chinese civil war, and of the signing of the Chinese–Soviet military alliance (in February 1950), Washington came to recognize Japan's potential value in the Cold War which was increasingly becoming militarized. American officials were coming to the view that a peace treaty with Japan should be concluded in such a way as to strengthen the US camp in the contest with the Soviet camp. Specifically, some US forces should remain in Japan, and especially in Okinawa, even after the termination of the occupation, and Japan itself should be encouraged to undertake rearmament so as to contribute to maintaining the military balance in the region. Of course, Soviet-bloc nations would refuse to agree to such a development, but American officials were prepared to hold a peace conference even without their participation. The US government had adopted such a position by May 1950 and dispatched John Foster Dulles to Tokyo to prepare the ground for a peace conference.

In Japan, there was fierce debate on the impending peace. Although the nation was still under US occupation, there was much open discussion over the issue of a 'total' versus 'partial' peace, that is, whether there should be a peace treaty to be signed by all former enemies of Japan, or one primarily with the United States and its Cold War partners. Several of the most prominent advocates of a 'total' peace were scholars primarily in Tokyo and Kyoto who organized a 'forum for the peace question'. As early as January 1950, they declared that Japan must insist on a total peace, pursue a policy of disarmament and neutrality, and refuse to have foreign military bases on its soil after regaining its independence. Such ideas reflected the spirit of the new constitution and had the support of the above-mentioned first group and part of the second group among the nation's opinion-leaders. Their basic assumption was that the Cold War did not define everything in the world and that Japan could make a contribution to world peace by maintaining itself as an unarmed, unmilitarized nation. Highly idealistic, this view was even then a minority view.

The majority of Japanese who expressed themselves on the peace question would seem to have agreed with the government's contention that against the reality of the Cold War it was practically impossible to realize a total peace, however desirable it might be in the abstract, and that if

111

Japan were to seek to terminate a foreign occupation, it must be prepared to accept a partial peace treaty with the United States and several other former enemies. They assumed that given the Cold War, Japan really had only two alternatives, either to side with the United States or with the Soviet Union. Opting for the former alternative entailed a willingness, according to this perspective, to enter into a security arrangement with the United States and even to undertake Japanese rearmament. Few, however, had pushed these ideas vigorously before the outbreak of the Korean war. For one thing, this option would foreclose any possibility of a peace settlement with the People's Republic of China. But there was considerable domestic opinion in favour of friendly relations with the PRC, especially among those who did not completely accept postwar Japan's orientation towards the United States and Western Europe. Even the government, while it had no diplomatic autonomy and thus was unable to define a policy towards the new China, retained a strong interest in promoting trade between the two countries. In such a perspective, it would be desirable to obtain Chinese participation in the forthcoming peace conference. These circumstances explain why the partial peace view was not yet a national consensus.

All this changed, however, with the North Korean assault on the south, in June 1950. The influence of realists, arguing for a partial peace treaty and even for rearmament, increased rapidly. Already in July, Ashida Hitoshi, a former prime minister, expressed his opinion in *Bungei shunjū* (Literary miscellany) that 'in the current situation, Japan must decide to which side of the divided world it belongs'. As noted earlier, he had, even before the Korean war, advocated rearmament for Japan, but he now argued that the new developments clearly indicated the pre-eminence of military force as the key determinant of international affairs. There could be no way Japan could safeguard its security while remaining unarmed and neutral. Many who had not shared Ashida's views on rearmament were now more receptive and willing to accept the option of a partial peace. To the extent that postwar Japan became re-militarized, therefore, the Korean war provided the immediate background.

Thus in August 1950 a new armed force of 75,000 men was created as ordered by the occupation authorities. It was called a police reserve corps, not exactly a fully-fledged army. Its primary task was to maintain domestic order, but it was expected that in time it would become a regular armed force and be called upon to safeguard national security. Such a corps impressed its critics as a clear violation of the new constitution's 'no war' clauses; but the government did not decide to revise the constitution before establishing such a force. Instead, it argued that the constitution had not prohibited the nation's 'right of self-defence'. This sort of semantic 'realism' would be resorted to more than once as Japan steadily augmented its armed power. At the same time, it may be noted that the very fact that the constitution remained unchanged served to place certain limitations upon Japanese rearmament. So long as the 'no war' principle of the postwar constitution was kept intact, the government could (and did) argue that the Japanese armed force was for purely defensive purposes and would never engage in an aggressive war or be sent overseas. Public opinion polls at that time indicated that the majority of those polled supported the establishment of a new armed force so long as it was kept within the country. In other words, the Japanese public at the time of the Korean war appears to have accepted limited rearmament within the framework of the constitution.

The outbreak of the Korean war made it more likely than ever that the peace treaty would be a partial one. Such 'realism' matched the US initiatives in late 1950 and early 1951, as Washington stepped up its preparations for a peace conference now that the Asian balance of power had been undermined by what appeared to be the Soviet-backed aggression committed by North Korea. American officials were convinced that a peace treaty with Japan must be accompanied by a security arrangement, for otherwise Japan, after the termination of the US occupation, would only invite Soviet expansionism. In a world defined by the Cold War, there could be no such thing as a neutral, unarmed Japan. Thus reasoning, American officials seized the opportunity provided by the Korean war to plan for a Japanese peace conference, which was convened in San Francisco in September 1951. In US policy, the restoration of Japanese sovereignty (except Okinawa, which was to remain under US control until 1972), Japan's rearmament, and the continued presence of US forces in Japan were all integral parts of the new Asian strategy. Because the second strand of this three-fold strategy, Japanese rearmament, was expected to take time, it was considered imperative to retain bases and facilities in Japan after the peace treaty was signed so as to contribute to restoring regional balance after it had been upset by the North Korean attack.

From the Soviet Union's standpoint, all this was clearly unacceptable. Just like the United States, it, too, viewed the question of the Japanese peace treaty in the context of the Cold War. Thus it was not surprising that it should have refused to sign the San Francisco peace treaty, or that the People's Republic of China should have also rejected the treaty. (Neither the PRC nor Taiwan was represented at the peace conference.) The United States, in the meantime, still viewed the Nationalist regime in Taiwan as the legitimate government of China and, accordingly, insisted that Japan should sign a peace treaty with that government.

Japanese behaviour at that time is interesting. The Yoshida cabinet clearly opted to sign a US-initiated peace treaty and followed it up by agreeing to a mutual security arrangement with the United States. Japanese public opinion seems to have supported such an approach. Unwilling to remove the nation from the Cold War framework or to promote a totally different framework of international relations, the Japanese saw no alternative to accepting the international system as defined by the United States and to seeking its security within that system. Opinion surveys at that time always indicated that more people supported a partial peace than a total peace. Regarding Japanese rearmament, however, the Yoshida cabinet insisted on a lower level of military power than the United States envisaged. Yoshida wanted to hold down defence expenditures and to rely on the United States to make up for whatever Japan itself could not provide. This essentially meant that Japanese military force would be used for the maintenance of domestic law and order, and that US support would be needed to cope with any external threat to Japan's security. Such a stance, Yoshida was convinced, would prevent the resurgence of militarism. Thus even when, in 1952, the police reserve corps was renamed the peace preservation force, he took pains to distinguish it from the prewar armed forces. Regarding China, too, the Yoshida cabinet took pains to ensure that any peace treaty it entered into with the Nationalist regime in Taiwan, in accordance with US wishes, would apply only to territory the latter controlled. In other words, Tokyo left open the possibility of some day signing another peace treaty with the People's Republic of China.

Considering the fact that this was the time when US forces were clashing with Chinese in Korea, even this degree of self-assertiveness was remarkable. As will be seen, while the Japanese were willing to identify their defence posture with that of the United States, they were also anxious to promote economic and cultural exchanges with the China mainland. In any event, thus was created the 'San Francisco system' of Asian international affairs, incorporating Japan together with South Korea, Taiwan, the Philippines, Australia, and New Zealand, to match the military power of the Soviet Union, China, and North Korea. The militarization of international relations had come to Asia by 1952.

Although the Cold War confrontation between the United States and the Soviet Union tended to accentuate the military factor in international relations, pushing to the background economic and other dimensions, these latter were by no means absent. For instance, Britain, a staunch ally of the United States, departed from the American policy towards the People's Republic of China and recognized the new Beijing (Peking) regime, conducting small-scale trade with it. Such an example shows that international military and economic affairs were not entirely interchangeable. Likewise, international cultural or intellectual affairs managed to survive in the margins of the military confrontation, as can be seen in the continuation, if tenuous, of scholarly exchanges between East- and West-bloc nations.

Japan was no exception. Indeed, its economic policy was not exactly in line with the Cold War strategy of the United States. Washington's primary objective in the economic realm was to make use of Japan's potential economic resources for regional stabilization. American officials were particularly interested in promoting close economic ties between Japan and Southeast Asia. Japan could expand its trade with the region, selling its products there and obtaining foodstuffs and raw materials in return. In a sense, Southeast Asia would play the role China did before the war for the Japanese economy. Because the United States did not want close economic ties between mainland China and Japan, the promotion of such ties between Japan and Southeast Asia seemed to make sense. At the same time, the United States offered Japan substantial economic assistance. Although not as large-scale as the Marshall aid in Europe, such assistance was envisaged as a long-term project, not just a temporary arrangement as part of the occupation policy. It is notable, for instance, that in 1950, of Japan's total imports of about $1 billion, fully one-third took the form of goods brought in from the United States as economic aid. The United States also took the initiative to approach its European allies to enable Japan after its independence to join the Bretton Woods system of international economic affairs. Thanks to such help, Japan was given membership of the World Bank, enabling it to borrow money from the bank for the construction of thermal power plants.

By far the most effective 'aid' rendered to Japan, however, was the so-called 'special procurement orders' during the Korean war. United States forces involved in the war altogether purchased some $500 million worth of food, clothing, medicine, and other items from Japan. Considering the fact that Japan's national income in 1950 was only $9.4 billion (or about one-twenty-third of America's), such a windfall was extremely significant, enabling the Japanese economy to regain the prewar level. (In real terms, Japan's gross national product regained the 1937 level only in 1952.) Japanese trade, too, began to grow. Already in 1950, both its exports ($827 million) and imports ($967 million) exceeded the figures for China, and the gap continued to widen, and Japan easily regained its position as the most important trading nation in Asia. But its trade deficits did not disappear. In 1952, for instance, Japanese import trade ($2.3 billion) was more than 50 per cent larger than export trade ($1.3 billion). The deficit was due to a great extent to the need to import large quantities of raw materials necessary for rapid industrialization. It was all the more necessary, therefore, to continue to receive US aid. (Japan was not to record a trade surplus till 1965.)

At the same time, however, such figures reveal why the Japanese were eager to promote trade with the China mainland. In order to expand its export so as to reduce trade deficits, Southeast and South Asian markets did not seem enough. China retained its attractiveness, even when it was fighting against the United States and thus Japanese–Chinese trade was of necessity a very limited one. Still, in 1951, the bilateral trade reached some $200 million, or 6 per cent of total Japanese trade and 10 per cent of Chinese. Although not as substantial as their prewar trade, there was the expectation that these modest beginnings would in time develop into something far more impressive. At least for the Japanese at that time, next to the United States and Southeast Asia, China was an important market, and they had no intention of giving it up just because they placed their country in the US camp in the Cold War. Of course, Japan had to abide by the restrictions imposed by COCOM (the Coordinating Committee for Export Control). More-over, at the end of 1950 the United States issued a total ban on trade with China, and as an indirect consequence of it Japanese trade with China shrank during 1951–52. Nevertheless, it never disappeared during the remainder of the Korean war. Indeed, as soon as the peace treaty went into effect in 1952, Japan and China signed a trade agreement. In June of that year, a private organization in Japan concluded the agreement with its counterpart in China. The fiction of a private arrangement had to be maintained in the absence of a formal relationship between Tokyo and Beijing. In any event, the fact that Japan was under US security protection did not prevent it from seeking to expand its trade relations with China, which was then fighting a war with Japan's ally. Although such relations were never powerful enough to alter the nature of the US–Japanese security arrangement, they did indicate the belief in Japan that its post-occupation foreign affairs would entail far more than security issues.

On the other hand, in the cultural or intellectual sphere, American influence was paramount. The trend had, of course, started in 1945, but it would seem to have picked up momentum after 1949. In part this was because, during the early Cold War, Japanese contact with the Soviet Union and China became attenuated. There were even 'red purges', involving the purging of those who had till then been tolerated, even supported, by the occupation authorities, such as labour union leaders, left-leaning professors, and communists. Japanese opinion inevitably shifted towards pro-US, non-radical, and conservative perspectives. But this was not all; Americanization not in such a narrow sense but as a more comprehensive phenomenon also was under way. We must remember that for more than ten years the Japanese had not had much contact with currents of American thought and scholarship. Now, however, they became cognizant of trends in American literature, arts, and scholarship (especially in the social sciences). These, coupled with films, baseball, and other cultural products, entered Japan as representatives of the American way of life. Because, at that time, American intellectual and cultural leaders were keenly conscious of their confrontation with communism, there was something of a missionarizing fervour about the outflow of American culture towards Japan and other countries.

All this seems to have further oriented Japanese opinion in the direction of the United States. A *Yomiuri* survey of the summer of 1950 showed that 65.7 per cent of those polled named the United States as the country they liked most. In April 1951 the same newspaper reported that 92.8 per cent of respondents said General MacArthur 'had been beneficial to Japan'. The generally popular occupation reforms, coupled with the influx of American influence, were having a distinctive impact on Japanese thought. This trend must have been confirmed by the Korean war; when in December 1950 *Yomiuri* asked if China's entry into the war increased the threat to Japanese security, 55.8 per cent answered in the affirmative, whereas only 22.7 per cent disagreed. Such a situation was making it more difficult to continue to hold a pro-Chinese or a neo-Asianist attitude. The 'total peace' advocates stuck to their position that Japan must develop close and unrestricted trade and other types of relations with China and other Asian countries, but public opinion was turning against such views. It is interesting to note that even American 'realism' in international relations theory was making its appearance in Japan.

For example, Koizumi Shinzō, one of the senior advisers

to the emperor, wrote in *Bungei shunjū* that against the reality of the US–Soviet confrontation, Japan had no choice but to safeguard its security through an agreement with the United States, unless it was prepared to augment its armed forces. Nomura Kichisaburō, prewar ambassador to Washington, argued on the pages of *Chūōkōron* that this was no time to indulge in abstract argument for or against the United States or the Soviet Union; instead, the Japanese must realize that their security was being steadily endangered. They must, therefore, 'request that the United States retain its forces in Japan for national security' even after the signing of the peace treaty. 'It makes sense to offer the use of our land to the nation that is going to protect us', he wrote. Public opinion seems to have supported such views; *Yomiuri* reported in August 1950 that 46.4 per cent of those polled expressed 'hope that American forces will remain in Japan'. In March 1951 the ratio had increased to 63.7 per cent.

At the same time, in non-defence matters, too, American cultural influence was growing. Even while the country was still occupied by US forces, a sizeable number of Japanese intellectuals and students were being invited, under the GARIOA programme, to study in American universities and schools. Nearly 1,000 Japanese students seem to have visited the United States before the peace treaty went into effect in 1952. The July 1951 issue of *Sekai*, to take an example, included articles on the theme of 'Returning from America', written by Japanese who reported on what they had witnessed in the United States, its current thought, social movements, educational system, and the like. Some reported on pacifism which was still in existence in American society, but this did not constitute an important part of the emerging Japanese knowledge of contemporary America. Japan's pacifists, therefore, were more likely to be critical of the United States than joining forces with pacifists in America. In any event, it seems clear that by 1952 America was becoming the most important country for Japan, strategically, economically, and culturally. Whether this was going to be a long-term trend or not, however, was not yet certain.

Chapter 10

THE ORIGINS OF PEACEFUL COEXISTENCE

How can we characterize the years between 1952, when Japan achieved independence, and 1960, when a new security treaty was concluded with the United States? At one level, of course, the military confrontation between the United States and the Soviet Union intensified throughout the 1950s; but, at the same time, the decade also witnessed the emergence of the idea of peaceful coexistence as well as the self-assertiveness of the so-called Third World. In other words, the 1950s saw both the intensification of the Cold War and moves to ease world tensions. Japanese foreign affairs were conducted in such an environment.

To begin with, there is little doubt that the military aspect of the Cold War became more and more serious, as both sides continued to build their respective arsenals. For instance, the United States possessed about 450 nuclear warheads in 1950, but the number increased to 18,500 by 1960. The Soviet Union hardly had any before 1955, but had accumulated over 3,000 warheads by the end of the decade. Corresponding to such increases, the two superpowers' military budgets continued to grow. (In 1963, the US defence expenditures amounted to $52.2 billion, and the Soviet Union's to $54.7 billion.) When, in 1957, the Soviet Union launched the earth satellite Sputnik, it heralded the coming of the age of missiles. From now on, nuclear weapons would not have to be carried by and dropped from aeroplanes; they could be fired from land bases or from vessels at sea. The United States quickly caught up in missile development, manufacturing Atlas and Titan missiles, the combined total of which exceeded the

Soviet arsenal by 1960, despite much talk of a 'missile gap' in American political circles.

Inevitably, there grew misgivings about such an arms race. Already at the end of the 1950s, President Eisenhower had warned that the United States alone had enough nuclear weapons to destroy the Western hemisphere, suggesting awareness that the nuclear weapons development had reached a stage where, in addition to maintaining some sort of balance between the superpowers, the very survival of humanity could be endangered. Many in the United States (and quite possibly in the Soviet Union as well) began wondering if nuclear arms were still to be useful and, if not, why they continued to be produced. Such thinking led to an idea of limited war, a war in which conventional arms and tactical nuclear weapons, not strategic nuclear weapons, would be used. The development of this idea was another interesting aspect of the 1950s. Indeed, throughout the decade, the United States and the Soviet Union not only refrained from using nuclear weapons against each other, but also began fighting 'proxy wars', in which covert means and political intrigue played important roles. Events in Iran in 1953, Guatemala in 1954, or Iraq in 1958 indicated that the bipolar confrontation involved not just military arms but local political struggles.

Nevertheless, the fundamental fact remains: international relations in the 1950s were defined by the military confrontation of the two superpowers. In that decade, the confrontation covered many regions of the world besides Europe, and the entire world became militarized. The admission of West Germany into NATO in 1955 led to its armament. In Eastern Europe, the Warsaw Pact was organized in 1955, perpetuating the presence of Soviet forces. In the Middle East, the Baghdad Pact was formed in the same year by Turkey and Iraq, to which Britain, Iran, and Pakistan adhered. (Iraq defected in 1959.) Elsewhere, the Southeast Asian Treaty Organization (SEATO) was established by the United States, Britain, the Philippines, and others; the United States also entered into bilateral security pacts with Taiwan and with South Korea. The Soviet Union, for its part, continued to uphold its alliances with China, North Korea, and North Vietnam, and after 1960 it began extending military assistance to the new, socialist regime of Cuba. Under such circumstances, it was not surprising that the world in 1960 appeared to be pregnant with grave dangers of war. The shooting down of a U-2 'spy plane' over Soviet territory in May that year, which led to the cancellation of a planned meeting between the US and Soviet heads of government, gave the impression that World War Three was just round the corner. It did not come, but there persisted crises over Berlin, Cuba, Laos, and elsewhere, inevitable consequences of the militarization of the globe.

At the same time, however, we should recognize that after the end of the Korean war, there was no other comparable war anywhere for the rest of the decade. Local conflicts persisted, but none with the magnitude of the Korean war. This fact, coupled with the continued arms race, characterized the 1950s. In other words, the militarization of international relations proceeded with its own momentum, without any clear relationship to actual events. Armaments were kept up when in reality neither US nor Soviet arms were utilized; their augmented arsenals did not bring war closer to reality. Thus military power defined but did not explain international affairs. There was a widening gap between the reality of military power and the realities of international relations. Under the circumstances, there inevitably arose a movement to check the tendency towards global militarization and to redefine international affairs in a framework other than that of US–USSR military confrontation. This was another important characteristic of the 1950s.

First of all, the term 'peaceful coexistence' began to be used in the Soviet Union after Stalin's death in 1953, and in the United States, too, some started speaking of 'a truce in the Cold War'. What such expressions suggested was the growing recognition that, despite the two superpowers' continued arms build-ups, their nuclear armament might not necessarily lead to war. At that time, neither power was willing to take steps to reduce its armaments and to establish a more peaceful relationship, but at least it seemed possible, and desirable, to grope for a definition of international relations that was not interchangeable with militarization. Peaceful coexistence emphasized the idea that in an increasingly militarized world, war was not inevitable – at least that efforts should be made to prevent war. Such thinking was reminiscent of the classical balance-of-power thought, but while the traditional balance of power could always break down, thus making international relations that much more unstable, the new peaceful coexistence idea was more complex, and more abstract in that it was seeking a peaceful alternative to nuclear armament even while the arms build-up continued. More specifically, it was believed possible to develop non-military ties, such as economic and cultural interchanges, between the two power blocs. None could predict how such a world, characterized at one level by militarization and at another by economic and cultural contact, would look, and whether this would ultimately end the US–Soviet confrontation. But even if the two powers' hegemonic position in world affairs might not be altered, it seemed worth pursuing these other paths as well. Such thinking was behind Vice-President Richard Nixon's trip to the Soviet Union in July 1959, or Chairman Nikita Khrushchev's trip to the United States two months later.

How such contacts would translate into a new pattern of US–Soviet relations was not at all clear. For instance, in 1956, when Poles and Hungarians rose up against Soviet domination of their countries and were suppressed brutally by Soviet military force, the United States did not intervene. This may have been an instance of peaceful coexistence; the episodes indicated a superpower's unwillingness to interfere with the affairs of another superpower in its sphere of influence, even while both sought to strengthen their respective alliance systems. Increased commercial and cultural contact might mean Poles and Hungarians were coming under increasing Western influence, but the Soviet Union would not tolerate such a situation developing into political instability and creating a challenge to the solidarity of the Eastern bloc. This was clearly a negative instance of the application of peaceful coexistence. At the same time, however, the superpowers *were* becoming interested in negotiating a ban on nuclear testing. Preliminary talks started in 1958. No formal agreement was to be reached till five years later, and neither side was seriously interested in nuclear arms reduction. But the prohibition or at least curtailment of tests was considered the first necessary step in that direction. In that sense, peaceful coexistence could potentially transform the military dimension of the Cold War.

The second important characteristic of world affairs during the 1950s was the emergence of the Third World as a significant factor. The control of nuclear testing, for instance, was an idea then vigorously promoted by India, Indonesia, and other new states, which had attained their independence only recently. They refused to identify themselves with either side in the Cold War and, instead, insisted on the need to establish an alternative international order. Often referred to as neutralism, these nations' interest was far more than just taking no side in the global confrontation; they wanted to transform international relations into something drastically different. These countries – most of them created from the old empires in Asia and Africa – were quite self-conscious about not being part of the Western world. They insisted that the Cold War definition of world affairs was little more than an extension of the traditional Western-centred diplomacy, whether the balance of power or imperialism.

What should they seek in place of the existing international order? One solution was 'the Bandung system', so called after the conference of Asian and African states in Bandung, Indonesia, in 1955. As many as twenty-nine countries attended, and the participants adopted a ten-part declaration on peace, in addition to calling on the superpowers to end their atomic tests, reduce armaments, and increase economic assistance.

The 'ten principles of peace' were derived from the 1954 Chinese–Indian declaration on 'five principles of peace', and stressed such themes as peaceful coexistence and non-interference in internal affairs of nations. There was nothing 'Third World' about such objectives, and neither the United States nor the Soviet Union could have taken exception to them in principle. But the very fact that Third World countries assembled together, to represent 'one-half of the entire world's population', as Sukarno said, was important. They were serving notice that no crucial development in the world could or should take place that ignored their voices. And for these people, the most critical issue was 'nation-building', especially economic development. To assist nation-building efforts, the Western powers should not only maintain a peaceful international environment but should reduce their arms so that what they saved thereby could be extended as economic assistance to these new states. To persist in militarization, in such a perspective, was to defy the dreams of the vast majority of humanity. In giving expression to this view, the Bandung conference marked an important stage in postwar history, the first serious critique by the Third World of the world order defined by the Cold War.

It is important to note that while India, Indonesia, and Egypt were among the leaders pushing for a Bandung alternative to the Cold War, China, too, joined forces with them. Although it had signed a treaty of alliance with the Soviet Union in 1950, at least in the mid-1950s its foreign policy was flexible enough to accommodate support for the Bandung agendas. China cooperated closely with India in Bandung, and it even called upon the United States to redefine the two countries' relations on the basis of peaceful coexistence. China's military spending, which had accounted for over 40 per cent of annual budgets during the Korean war, fell to 19 per cent by 1957. If these and other participants at Bandung had remained united for a little longer, international relations might indeed have been redefined, away from the bipolar confrontation. In reality, however, the Cold War definition of world affairs was not fundamentally altered by the Bandung initiative. The United States and the Soviet Union continued to conduct their foreign affairs as if Bandung had not happened; their peaceful coexistence diplomacy was carried on quite regardless of Third World initiatives.

The basic reason for the failure of the Bandung conference to affect international affairs seriously was that the Third World was unable to stay united. China, for instance, abandoned peaceful coexistence by 1958 and once again adopted a sharply anti-US stance, as witnessed by its attacks on the 'offshore islands' (Quemoy and Matsu). Beijing expected Moscow to come to its assistance during the crisis, apparently even willing to risk chances of a US–Soviet confrontation over the islands. This degree of belligerence was unacceptable to the Soviet leadership under Khrushchev and led ultimately to a split in the alliance. Whereas at Bandung China and India had cooperated, their relations deteriorated over the border question, which even led to war in 1962. In the Middle East, too, neutrality tended to be forsaken for an identification with either side in the Cold War. Thus Egypt and Iraq inclined towards the Soviet Union, while Lebanon sought US military assistance.

All such developments meant that the spirit of Bandung did not last long, and that it was unable to do much about global militarization. Nevertheless, one should note the forceful assertion, by the Bandung participants, of the idea that economics, especially the economic development of newly independent states, should be the basis for a more peaceful and stable international order. The idea was not yet of decisive importance, but it would retain its influence through the subsequent decades, to re-emerge powerfully through the United Nations and other world agencies in the 1970s and the 1980s.

To respond to the challenge, the advanced countries proposed their own ideas of modernization and economic development. These ideas, too, constituted an important legacy of the 1950s. As developed in the United States and Western Europe, the modernization theory was still couched in the large framework of the Cold War; it was asserted that through assisting the economic development and other modernization schemes of Asian, African, and Latin American countries – collectively called 'underdeveloped nations' – the West would be able to prevent them from falling into the Soviet camp. The ideology of 'liberal developmentalism' pitted itself against Marxism and revolutionary anti-imperialism, asserting that non-revolutionary paths towards modernization existed and, therefore, that the capitalist and underdeveloped nations should be able to forge a mutually beneficial, inter-dependent relationship. Economic development would, it was believed, lead to political democratization; and since democratic regimes would be by definition pro-Western, the advanced nations should do all they could to assist modernization programmes in underdeveloped areas of the world. Liberal developmentalist ideology juxtaposed itself to the reigning ideology of the Cold War confrontation, but the two were not considered to be at odds. Rather, the former constituted a part of the latter ideology. In that sense, the West's developmental ideology was not quite the same thing as the Third World's.

These were some of the main features of international relations when Japan regained its independence and set about the task of re-entering the international community. To be sure, the San Francisco peace treaty, which went into effect in April 1952, still left Japanese relations with the Soviet Union and the People's Republic of China in a state of war. But at least the formal occupation of Japan – with the exception of Okinawa – by US forces had ended, and Japan defined itself anew as a sovereign nation. As such, it was not surprising that its first task was to build up its defence capabilities. It is interesting, however, to contrast the military programmes of post-1952 Japan with those in the Meiji period. Japan's military strengthening had been considered the priority item of the Meiji government so that defence expenditures usually accounted for 20 to 30 per cent, sometimes even 40 per cent, of annual governmental outlays, whereas during 1952–60 military spending was only about 10 per cent of the budgets. In this period actual defence expenditures increased by 50 per cent, but the total governmental outlays doubled, so that the portion of military spending in the budget steadily decreased. On the other hand, portions to be allocated for education, culture, and social welfare equalled, and at times exceeded, defence spending, in sharp contrast to the Meiji practice.

To be sure, Japan could afford to spend proportionally less on defence because it was assisted by the United States. Gratuitous US military aid between 1951 and 1958 (when the programme was terminated) amounted to about $1.2 billion, enabling Japan to devote the bulk of its resources to economic and social programmes. Still, this was also a conscious decision on the part of the Japanese government. Not just Yoshida Shigeru but his successors, Hatoyama Ichirō, Ishibashi Tanzan, and even Kishi Nobusuke (despite his reputation as a hard-liner) shared the same perspective on defence. It should be noted that Japan in the 1950s was a far richer country than during the Meiji era. (The per capita income in 1900 was roughly $8, whereas in 1955 it was about $200. Of course, steep increases in commodity prices in these years must be taken into consideration, but even so incomes had grown faster.) In other words, it would have been theoretically possible to spend more on defence in the 1950s than a half century earlier. That this was not done was not just a reflection of the economic realities in post-independence Japan but a self-conscious decision by the leaders, and ultimately the Japanese people themselves. Popular opinion polls indicated that their perspectives on defence had not changed noticeably after 1952. The majority of them did not find limited armament incompatible with the new constitution, but at the same time they opposed constitutional revision to undertake a more substantial arms build-up. According to surveys undertaken by the Prime Minister's Office, 66 per cent of those polled in 1956, and 61 per cent in 1957, said that the country 'needs an armed force', but only 19 per cent in 1956 and 24 per cent in the following year supported a revision of the constitution. (26 per cent and 24 per cent of those surveyed in these years opposed constitutional revision, while the rest were undecided.) Japan's defence policy reflected such thinking. About 10 per cent of annual budgets would be earmarked for military expenditures, but Japan would not seek to become a military power, instead devoting most of its resources to economic and social well-being. This stance was maintained by the Liberal Democratic Party (LDP), formed in 1955 from two conservative political parties.

Even this degree of rearmament was opposed by those who had earlier advocated a 'total' peace treaty and by others identified with the pacifism of the 'peace problems forum', which continued its activities even after the signing of the peace treaty. They argued, first of all, that any armament was contrary to the spirit of the 'peace constitution'. Former Tokyo University President Nanbara Shigeru, for instance, wrote in the *Sekai* (World) monthly in 1955 that Japan after independence had abandoned the path of anti-militarism and peace so nobly declared in the constitution; instead, the nation was making preparations for another war. Japanese leaders 'were hastening to remilitarize Japan' in violation of the constitution which forbade armament. Such a situation was 'in a sense similar to that on the eve of the Pacific war'. The fear that Japan might be repeating the prewar road to disaster seemed vindicated when Kishi, who had been tried as a war criminal, became prime minister in 1957.

The opponents of governmental policy in addition asserted that Japan's decision to undertake rearmament was tantamount to accepting the Cold War as the only reality and to fitting the nation into the picture, instead of taking the initiative towards constructing a more peaceful international order. Japan must, Nanbara wrote, make a contribution to 'the relaxation of world tensions and the unity of mankind'. This was 'the new mission and ideal' of the Japanese people, who must 'eschew war, abolish armament, and transform their country into a peaceful and cultural nation'. Precisely because world affairs were characterized by the bipolar confrontation, the Japanese should try to help create a new reality in which the Cold War would be mitigated, while cultural exchanges and trade were promoted. The view that Japan should make a contribution to the international community, not through military means, but through culture, would, in two or three decades, come to have strong influence at home and abroad, but in the 1950s it was a minority opinion. Given the fact that military power was the major definer of international relations, to advocate an outright abolition of armaments was to offer an important antithesis which, however, had little prospect of being accepted anywhere.

Complete disarmament, then, was not to be Japan's choice. Instead, Tokyo opted for a policy of limited armament so that the nation's security would be sought through the combination of its own forces and the military power of the United States which would retain its bases in the country and continue to keep Okinawa under its jurisdiction. Limited armament for Japan, and reliance on US military power, were thus in a symbiotic relationship.

But there was some disagreement between Tokyo and Washington as to the level of Japanese armament. In 1953, when Ikeda Hayato, representing the LDP, and Walter S. Robertson, a State Department official, met in Washington, Robertson demanded that Japan should increase its armed strength to about 350,000 men. The Yoshida cabinet resisted the pressure and succeeded in scaling down Japan's military force to 110,000 men. They were organized into the new Self-Defence Force, on the basis of which the two nations signed a mutual defence assistance agreement (MSA) in

1954. Yoshida was replaced by Hatoyama later that year, but the new cabinet maintained the same defence policy. At the same time, however, the Hatoyama cabinet was interested in revising the 1951 mutual security pact, to make it more of an equal partnership than had been possible earlier. For instance, the pact had not specified that the United States had an obligation to protect Japan. Hatoyama wanted such an explicit guarantee. On Japan's part, he thought it would be necessary to revise the constitution to justify the defence build-up. In reality, however, neither the security treaty nor the constitution was altered at this time, and Japanese defence expenditures did not increase significantly. Because the basic policy on defence did not change, the Hatoyama cabinet was able then to turn to the problem of restoring diplomatic relations with the Soviet Union. As far as he was concerned, such overtures towards the Soviet Union were possible only because there already existed a firm defence pact with the United States. Unfortunately, however, the normalization of relations with Moscow proved very controversial in Japan and even led to the resignation of the cabinet.

Hatoyama was succeeded by Ishibashi as prime minister, but his leadership lasted but two months because of his illness. In December 1956 Kishi organized a new cabinet. He, too, basically continued the Yoshida legacy, although Japan's defence spending increased by about 7 per cent between 1957 and 1960. But defence spending as a portion of the total governmental outlays declined from 13 per cent in 1957 to 9 per cent in 1960, which corresponded to 1.9 per cent and 1.4 per cent of the national income in the respective years. This was because national income grew by 45 per cent during this period.

It was ironical that despite these facts, the Kishi cabinet was forced to resign in 1960 in the wake of the nationwide movement against the revision of the US–Japan security treaty. Unlike Hatoyama, Kishi did not consider it necessary to change the constitution in order to revise the security treaty, but he did want a clear statement that the United States was responsible for protecting the 'territory under the administration of Japan' from external attack. This certainly did not indicate an intention to undertake Japan's further militarization, as Kishi's critics argued. Still, from the opponents' point of view, the revision and renewal of the security treaty with the United States would perpetuate Japan's dependence on the United States in a world defined in terms of the Cold War. The type of thinking exemplified by the ideas of the above-mentioned Nanbara Shigeru was still evident, especially since it seemed as if Cold War tensions were abating, as witness Khrushchev's trip to the United States in 1959. On the other hand, when tensions once again heightened in the spring of 1960, following the shooting down of a U-2 reconnaissance aircraft, it seemed as if the Cold War was going to resume its seriousness. Under such circumstances, many Japanese felt their country should not risk becoming a target of Soviet retaliation by staying too close with the United States. Furthermore, Kishi's wartime background (he was minister of commerce and industry in the Tōjō cabinet) added to the impression that he was a 'reactionary' politician; at least, the Socialists and other opposition parties sought to bring down his cabinet by popularizing such a notion. When Kishi's LDP forced a passage of the new security treaty in the Lower House of the Diet just a month before President Eisenhower's planned visit to Japan, the cabinet was accused of having timed the ratification accordingly; in Japanese law, the treaty would come into effect after one month had elapsed from the day of ratification. Massive demonstrations were organized, denouncing not just the treaty but also Prime Minister Kishi's 'militarism' and 'anti-democratic' behaviour. Those involved in the movement reiterated time and again that they were not anti-US, but that they were intent on preventing Japan's remilitarization and protecting its democracy. Perhaps they were right, for, as soon as Kishi requested President Eisenhower to cancel his trip and assumed responsibility for the fiasco by resigning, the movement against the new security treaty fizzled out, allowing it to come into effect without much protest.

There was, however, another important aspect to the 1960 crisis. Opponents of the new security treaty with the United States feared that, because it strengthened military ties between the two countries, it would further complicate Japan's relations with the People's Republic of China, making it that much more difficult to effect normalization. Compared to the early 1950s, there were far stronger voices calling for a *rapprochement* with Beijing. This was in part a reflection of the two countries' trade which, despite the absence of a diplomatic relationship, had steadily grown. For instance, by 1956 Japan's trade with the PRC had come to exceed that with Taiwan. There were several reasons for this. For one thing, many Japanese believed that trade with Southeast Asian countries would not be sufficient for their economic recovery, and that Japan could never ignore the huge potential markets in China. Japan's overall export trade in 1952 amounted to about $1.3 billion, which increased to $2.8 billion by 1957. China's share in these amounts was 1 per cent and 2 per cent, respectively. To this one would have to add Japanese exports to Hong Kong, amounting to twice the volume of exports to the PRC, for part of the goods shipped to Hong Kong must have been sent on to the mainland. For China, going through the first five-year plan (1953–57), Japanese imports such as bicycles, typewriters, cameras, cotton spinning and weaving machines, and (after COCOM restrictions were relaxed) cranes and other industrial machinery played important roles in its domestic economy second only to Soviet imports.

The growth of the China trade, even as Japan relied on the United States for its security, was a good example of the policy of 'separation of politics and economics' which the Japanese government pursued. There could be no complete separation; COCOM restrictions, for instance, made sure that politics controlled economics. Nevertheless, both the Japanese government and business community were eager to promote trade with China and sought to have COCOM regulations modified with respect to that country. In a sense postwar Japan was reversing the order of priorities between 'strong army' and 'rich nation'. Before the war, the former was almost always given top billing, but in the wake of the regaining of its independence in 1952, the nation focused on economic recovery and growth. Its national income grew from $14.1 billion in 1952 to $33.3 billion eight years later. As if to certify such economic development, Japan became a full member of the Bretton Woods system. In 1955 the nation was admitted into GATT (the General Agreement on Tariffs and Trade) and into the IMF (International Monetary Fund). Indeed, the 1955 meeting of the GATT members took place in Tokyo. In such a situation, it was not surprising that voices clamoured for more extensive trade relations with China.

In addition, there was an ideological and cultural aspect to Japan's increasing interest in mainland China. Part of this was the traditional pan-Asianist sentiment, which was now reinforced by the ideology of anti-imperialism which many on the left held. For those who did not welcome postwar Japan's cultural orientation towards the United States, China appeared as an attractive alternative. For Japanese with a feeling of guilt about the past aggressions in China and with a sense of admiration for the accomplishments of Communist China, the government's continued adherence to the San Francisco framework of Japanese foreign affairs was unacceptable. Expressing such a perspective, Asanuma Inejirō, general secretary of the Socialist Party, declared in Beijing in March 1959 that 'American imperialism is the common enemy of Japan and China'. This was extreme language, but even those who did not go that far entertained the thought that an improvement in Japanese relations with China would help relax Cold War tensions and suggest an alternative approach to Japan's foreign policy.

The Chinese leaders, on their part, supported the expansion of contacts between the two peoples, in the expectation that such a trend in Japanese opinion would alienate Japan from its Pacific ally. As early as 1953, for instance, China welcomed the visit of a Japanese friendship mission headed by the businessman Ikeda Masanosuke, and two years later a group of scholarly and cultural figures, led by the famous novelist Kuo Mo-jo, visited Japan. Kuo stressed, in his talks with Tanizaki Jun'ichirō and other Japanese hosts, that the two countries had a long history of interactions. The implication was that, despite the tragedy of the war, the two sides could build a new relationship on the recognition of this history. Rōyama Masamichi, a prominent political scientist, echoed the same view, writing for *Sekai* in February 1957 that while 'the good relationship from time immemorial' between the two peoples had experienced 'an unnatural state' because of Japanese behaviour in China after the Manchurian crisis, the Communist leadership 'is not blaming such past behaviour on Japan's part but is desirous of establishing a friendly relationship on the basis of equality and mutuality'. Such overtures, he noted, could not but help 'arouse among the Japanese a moral sentiment in favour of renewing the historical ties' between the two countries. Based on such thinking, in 1956 the Japan–China Cultural Exchange Association was organized under the leadership of the literary critic Nakajima Kenzō to promote exchanges in scholarship, literature, music, art, and other fields between the two countries.

It is difficult to say how such ideas and activities affected the basic structure of Japanese foreign policy based on the American security treaty. Both in quantity and quality, Japanese cultural relations with the United States surpassed those with China. During 1952–60 some 2,500 Japanese students and young scholars went to the United States under the Fulbright programme, and another 500 or so studied in American colleges and universities. Kabuki troupes and artists began touring American cities, and a large number of American scholars, tourists, and businessmen – exceeding the number from China – came to Japan. Such cultural contact provided a solid basis for the security ties across the Pacific. Nevertheless, the resumption of Japanese cultural relations with China complicated the picture. There was a tension between Japan's relations with the United States and with China. Asanuma's above-mentioned speech was in a way exhorting his countrymen to give priority to China even at the expense of Japan's ties to the United States.

Against this background, the Kishi cabinet's foreign policy was to opt for the continuation of the American connection. This became clear after 1957, when the prime minister visited Taiwan (see below) and provoked the PRC's ire. The following year saw Tokyo–Beijing relations deteriorate in the aftermath of the Nagasaki flag incident in which a Japanese youth pulled down the Chinese flag at a China market fair, resulting in Beijing's decision to stop all trade with Japan. This coincided with the radicalization of China's domestic and foreign affairs, as seen in the launching of the Great Leap Forward campaign at home, aimed at increasing agricultural production through the formation of people's communes, and the attacks on 'offshore islands' such as Quemoy and Matsu. In contrast to

US–Soviet relations where peaceful coexistence had begun to be stressed, the Chinese leadership insisted on continued confrontation with American imperialism. Instead of the earlier adherence to 'the five principles of peace', Mao argued that 'the east wind is prevailing over the west wind'. Whatever the motive for the reintroduction of a strongly ideological element in Chinese foreign policy, this radicalization brought about a deterioration in China's relations with the United States, Japan, and ultimately the Soviet Union. Kishi's decision to negotiate for a new security treaty with the United States, then, reflected the judgement that, given the difficulty of maintaining good relations with both Washington and Beijing, it was important to reconfirm Japan's commitment to the US security system. For this decision, Kishi was attacked by the Socialists and other pro-China groups, while Japan's trade with mainland China, which had grown steadily through the 1950s, plummeted to near zero by 1959. It would be only in 1963 that trade between Japan and mainland China would return to the level attained in 1957.

Interestingly enough, it proved easier to restore normal relations with the Soviet Union. The Cold War was still the overarching framework of world affairs, but neither Washington nor Moscow viewed a Japan–USSR *rapprochement* as altering drastically that structure. Compared to the United States or China, no deep historical ties existed between Japan and the Soviet Union. Their trade was minimal, and the only important economic issue concerned Japanese fishing off Soviet coasts. Perhaps it was because the bilateral relationship was relatively unimportant that Tokyo and Moscow were able to come together and sign a normalisation agreement in 1956. Japanese officials expected that normalization would help solve such issues as the rights of Japanese fishermen in Soviet waters, the repatriation of Japanese prisoners of war still in Siberia, and Japanese membership in the United Nations (for which a unanimous vote by the permanent members of the Security Council was required). For Soviet officials, normalization would be necessary to settle the question of the status of what the Japanese would call 'northern territory', the islands off Hokkaido which Soviet forces had occupied since the war. Soviet policy on the territorial question was not always consistent. In 1956, when the two countries began talks for normalization, Moscow was willing to return Habomai and Shikotan, the two islands lying closest to Hokkaido, to Japan, leaving the question of the status of the two other northern islands (Etorofu and Kunashiri) for future negotiation. In 1960, however, as the Japanese–US security treaty was signed, the Soviet Union notified Tokyo that Habomai and Shikotan could not be returned to Japan till US forces were withdrawn from Japan, a unilateral declaration which was against the spirit and letter of the 1956 agreement, as Russian authorities later admitted. Still, the inconsistency in the Soviet Union indicated that it was not taking its relations with Japan very seriously. Likewise, on Japan's part, there was little direction beyond the 1956 agreement. Japan now had a diplomatic relationship with the Soviet Union and joined the United Nations, but beyond these steps, it was not clear how Tokyo intended to make use of them in developing its foreign policy.

The Kishi cabinet was likewise intent upon establishing normal relations with Asian countries with which Japan had fought or which its forces had occupied during the war. As soon as diplomatic relations with Moscow were restored, Kishi made a tour of Asian countries such as Burma, Indonesia, the Philippines, and India. He also visited Australia and New Zealand. One key question he could not avoid, especially in the countries Japan had occupied, was reparations, and Kishi started the process of settling the question with each Asian country so that by the 1970s reparations payments would be completed in all nations. But he had greater difficulty with regard to China and Korea. In 1957 he visited Taiwan, in part to convey his gratitude to the Nationalist government for its generosity; Chiang Kai-shek had declared in 1945 that China would not demand reparations from Japan. But the Communist leadership on the mainland did not recognize the validity of Chiang's promises, so that no settlement of the war would be complete until Japan dealt directly with the Beijing government. In the meantime, as noted above, Kishi's visit to Taiwan was viewed by Beijing as an expression of Japan's hostility towards the Communist government and brought about the cooling of Tokyo's relations with the mainland.

Kishi also had great difficulty in improving relations with

Korea. The Japanese government since 1952 had been interested in re-establishing relations with South Korea (the Republic of Korea), leaving aside the question of North Korea (the Democratic People's Republic of Korea). But no progress had been made before Kishi resigned in 1960. Japanese colonization, of course, had come to an end in 1945, and the San Francisco peace treaty had explicitly mentioned Korea's independence. So the problem now was what to do with the past. How should Japan apologize for its past rule in Korea? What should be done about the property left behind in Korea by Japanese who had been repatriated? What should be decided about the status of those Koreans who had been forcibly brought to Japan before 1945 and who had remained there after the war? On these issues the two governments had wide disagreement, particularly since they were related to the two countries' respective self-identities and perceptions of history. The fact that the question of Japan's apology for its colonial rule over Korea still agitates Japanese and Koreans in the 1990s may explain why it was so hard to deal with it in the 1950s. But the Japanese government did not help resolve the impasse by refusing to take an explicit stand on the history of colonization in Korea. One Japanese negotiator even made an insensitive remark in 1953 that there had been some good aspects to Japanese governance of Korea.

Such thoughtlessness reflected the absence of a clear ideological foundation of Japanese foreign policy, an explicit vision of the role the nation sought to play in the international community. Japan's security and trade policies were rather clear, but the government had failed to develop a vision of its position in international affairs, although some opinion leaders had been presenting their own perspectives, as noted above. To be sure, there was the rough idea that the war had been a disaster and that the nation was not going to become a military power again, instead devoting its energies to economic development. But beyond such an idea, efforts were lacking to define Japan's new role in the world. Thus there were inconsistencies in Japanese foreign affairs; for instance, whereas Japan attended the Bandung conference in 1955, it absented itself from further meetings of Asian and African nations. While it signed reparations agreements with Burma and the

Philippines, it did not do so with South Korea. The lack of a clear ideology or vision characterized Japanese diplomacy of the 1950s, something that it had in common with much of the history of prewar Japanese foreign relations.

Chapter 11

THE EMERGENCE OF THE THIRD WORLD

The world of the 1960s was characterized by both the culmination of the US–Soviet Cold War to its maximum limits, and the beginning of its erosion as the defining reality of international affairs. On one hand, the military confrontation between the two superpowers continued. The US nuclear arsenal reached its largest size in 1965 with about 32,000 warheads. The Soviet Union had fewer than half of this number, but by 1970 the gap had narrowed, with its 18,000 nuclear warheads, while the United States had reduced the size to 27,000. In 1965 the Soviet Union's military spending for the first time surpassed that of the United States. The two powers continued to enjoy a virtual monopoly of nuclear arms in the world. At the same time, however, they did not engage in a nuclear war; even as grave a situation in US–USSR relations as the Cuban missile crisis of 1962 did not result in a war between them. Thus the question that had arisen in the late 1950s became even more serious: why was it necessary for the superpowers to continue producing nuclear arms when they were not going to use them against each other?

One conclusion was that the very reality of 'mutually assured destruction' (MAD) – that the existing nuclear weapons were sufficient to destroy each other and the entire world – made nuclear war unlikely. Once that threshold had been reached, there would be no point in continuing to add to the existing nuclear arsenals. In such a situation, it would make little sense to focus on a nuclear strategy, whether offensive or defensive, as the linchpin of their respective defence policies. It was a step from such a logic to the acceptance by the two powers of some formal agreement on controlling the continued manufacturing and spreading of these weapons. Such thinking led to the 1963 partial nuclear test-ban treaty and the 1968 non-proliferation treaty. The 1963 treaty, while it did not cover all tests but banned only those conducted in the atmosphere, clearly reflected the MAD-type thinking, as did the 1968 treaty to prevent the spread of nuclear weapons, which both the United States and the Soviet Union were eager to achieve. By this time, then, it may be said that US–Soviet relations had reached an equilibrium. The militarization of international relations that had begun in 1949 had reached a certain conclusion and brought about a modicum of stability.

It was precisely at this moment that new challenges presented themselves, challenges that would create fresh problems both to the superpowers and to the whole world. First was the appearance of a fissure in the Atlantic alliance, as exemplified by France's refusal to sign either the 1963 or the 1968 treaty. The nation, under the leadership of Charles de Gaulle who returned to power in 1958, successfully conducted nuclear tests in 1960 and sought to develop independent foreign and military policies; thus, for instance, it withdrew from NATO's military arrangements (pulling French forces out of the NATO command), and de Gaulle openly criticized the US involvement in Southeast Asia.

Still, in Europe, the common fear of Soviet power kept the NATO allies together. The problem was more serious elsewhere, especially in Asia where China was emerging as a major military power. It, too, developed its own nuclear forces – its first tests took place in 1964 – and, like France, it did not sign the 1963 and 1968 treaties. China's military budget, while not made public, was estimated to have amounted to over $10 billion annually after 1963. Beijing also sought to extend its influence in the Third World, attacking US imperialism and Soviet 'revisionism' as incompatible with Asian and African people's struggle for liberation. From around 1968, anti-revisionism and anti-hegemonism became China's slogans, aimed against the superpowers and intent upon constructing a new international order separate from the one defined by those two. The result was increased tensions in China's relations both with the United States and with the Soviet Union. In 1969, indeed, Chinese and Soviet forces clashed twice along the Siberian border.

Even more ominous were the wars that erupted in the periphery, away from the two global power centres. China and India fought a war in 1962, India and Pakistan in 1965, Israel and its Arab neighbours in 1967. In 1965 Indonesia severed ties with China, accusing the latter of interference in its internal affairs. All these episodes suggested that, even as the possibility of nuclear war faded, local wars increased in frequency. Why should this have been the case? Fundamentally, it reflected the coming into existence of many new states outside of Europe and the Western hemisphere. These new states were no more immune from mutual conflict than the Western nations had been earlier, and like them the new states' foreign affairs were closely connected to domestic politics. Many of them had gained independence only a decade or two earlier, and their political systems had remained unstable. Often these states had loosely defined territorial boundaries. At the same time, the leadership and populace in all countries were extremely nationalistic. All these created conditions rife for complicated external relations. Precisely because a third world war appeared less likely now, small-scale clashes and wars became more frequent.

The US war in Vietnam, the longest and costliest war of the 1960s, does not, at one level, fit into such a picture. Here was a nuclear giant waging war against a new state which, however, had not become a fully independent entity. Indeed, it was precisely the Vietnamese nationalists' struggle to create a unified nation that put them in opposition to the United States which was intent upon keeping two Vietnams separate. Washington's policy-makers applied to the situation some of the guiding concepts of the Cold War – 'containment', 'domino theory', 'credibility' – which were becoming less relevant in view of the US–USSR stabilization. Despite the massive involvement of US forces, who fought against the Vietcong in the south and attacked targets in the north, the policy proved unworkable. It was impossible to maintain South Vietnam as a separate entity; it became less and less a state than an existence whose government could last only so long as US forces protected it. In the end, American policy-makers judged this was an untenable position, especially since few of their allies abroad – with the conspicuous exception of South Korea – gave the United States full support for the Southeast Asian war. The principle of 'credibility', in other words, was very important in waging a Cold War against the Soviet Union but not a local conflict. As for the 'containment' strategy, not only did the United States fail to prevent China and the Soviet Union from assisting North Vietnam (short of provoking US retaliation), but the United States itself abandoned the policy in favour of a *rapprochement* with the PRC.

This abrupt shift in US–PRC relations was formalized in the 1970s, but in a way it was a logical outcome both of the changes in the superpower relationship and of the intensification of local wars. The former had brought about the alienation of China simultaneously from Washington and Moscow, but Beijing's leaders judged that the latter was a greater menace for the time being, especially after the Soviet invasion of Czechoslovakia in 1968 to crush the democratization movement. As for the United States, the Vietnam war indicated the limits of what it could do to influence developments in the periphery. One of the first policy statements made by Richard Nixon who became president in 1969 was the Guam doctrine which asserted that the nation would henceforth desist from military involvement in Asian wars and turn to Asians themselves to maintain regional order. That included Chinese, and the Nixon administration began relaxing travel restrictions to the mainland. It was no accident that international relations of the 1960s began with the Cuban missile crisis and ended with the initiation of steps towards bringing about a US–PRC *rapprochement*. Both suggested the passing of a phase in world affairs fundamentally defined by the superpower confrontation and the coming of a far more complex set of new issues.

The new issues, however, were not simply military or strategic. There were impressive developments in the 1960s in the economic and cultural spheres as well. Economically, the Bretton Woods system of multilateral commerce continued to function, and the decade saw impressive increases in world trade. The index of trade volume, taking 1913 as the base year (100), rose to 153 by 1953 and 269 by 1962. In other words, whereas during 1913–53 world trade had increased by only 50 per cent, during the next ten years it expanded by over 70 per cent. There were further increases in the trade index, to 407 in 1968 and 520 in 1971, suggesting that the 1960s were a remarkable decade in the history of international commerce. Moreover, not just the United States but many other countries recorded impressive increases. United States trade (export and import combined) jumped from $35.2 billion to $113.6 billion during the 1960s, but the rates of increase of Japanese and West European trade were even higher. The United States welcomed such a trend and took the initiative, through the Kennedy Round, to negotiate agreements with other countries to reduce mutual tariffs. These negotiations, begun in 1962, were successfully concluded in 1967.

The United Nations defined the 1960s as 'the decade of development', having in view the determination of Third World countries to undertake economic development. The expansion of world-wide trade would, it was considered, benefit the Third World and facilitate its development. Unfortunately, the trade of Third World countries did not grow as rapidly as that of the advanced countries, so that where in the 1950s Third World exports accounted for one-fourth of total world exports, the ratio had shrunk to one-fifth by the 1960s. Because the developing countries' rates of growth were lower than those among the developed nations, the gap between the two groups widened. Precisely for this reason, development became an overriding concern of Third World countries.

How should the nations of the world spend the increasing incomes that were becoming theirs, thanks to economic growth and trade expansion? It is interesting to note that in most countries the ratio of military spending to GNP remained steady in the 1960s, suggesting that they were spending more and more on military power. Ultimately, this could lead to a situation where even expanding economies would be unable to finance costly defence expenditures. Ironically, the United States, the richest country in the world, exemplified this problem because of its involvement in Vietnam. Its GNP was roughly $503 billion in 1960, and $982 billion ten years later. Vietnam war expenditures in 1969 alone totalled $26.3 billion, and sometimes as much as $100 million was spent in a day. Even for the United States, the war was becoming unmanageably expensive. But the Kennedy and the Johnson administrations were confident that the nation could pay for the war through economic growth (which would bring more governmental revenue) rather than through increased taxes – till 1968, when the administration finally decided to increase the income tax. But by then fiscal deficits were reaching serious proportions. For instance, in 1968, there was a deficit of $19.8 billion, part of which had to be financed through printing more money. This led to inflation; whereas at the beginning of the Kennedy administration, the rate of inflation was a mere 1 or 2 per cent, by the end of the Johnson administration it had crept up to 5 per cent. Such a situation inevitably weakened the dollar in the foreign exchange market, making it difficult already by 1966 to maintain the value of the dollar in terms of gold ($35 per ounce) which had been maintained under the Bretton Woods system. Americans turned increasingly to imported goods which were relatively cheaper, but foreign countries were losing their confidence in the value of the dollar. They wanted to exchange their dollar reserves for gold, or for other stronger currencies such as the German mark or the French franc. This put further pressure on the dollar as the international medium of exchange.

In a sense the relative weakening of the dollar at the end of the 1960s symbolized the passing of the age of American economic hegemony. In this sense, too, the end of the 1960s and the beginning of the 1970s were a turning point in postwar history. The United States, the richest and strongest power, was devoting its resources on a costly war, while other advanced countries remained uninvolved, instead concentrating on economic growth. This, plus economic development in Third World countries, suggested the emergence of new themes in international affairs.

A parallel development in the cultural sphere underscored the significance of the 1960s. The 'counter-culture' and 'new left' movements in the United States and elsewhere became visible and influential from around 1964 and directly challenged the hitherto prevailing social orders and mainstream ideologies. Although these movements had much to do with the growing resistance to the Vietnam war, they eventually produced a cultural force opposed to the establishment. Not just intellectuals but other segments of American society promoted the anti-establishment cultures, which quickly resonated elsewhere in the world. In international affairs, the movement had the effect of weakening the ideological basis of the Cold War. To be sure, many opponents of the Vietnam war did not initially question the premises of the global confrontation with the Soviet Union, but in time the Cold War itself came to be subjected to serious reconsideration. The 'new left' and 'revisionists' argued that the Vietnam fiasco was but a product of the mentality and strategy that had sustained the Cold War, and that the only way to end the war was by changing the ideology and strategy that had underlain the global confrontation, such as the geopolitical definition of international affairs, the dualistic conception of the world that was seen to be divided into forces of good and of evil, or the assumption that American ideas and values were universally valid. By assaulting these assumptions and attitudes, the critics were attacking not just US foreign policy but also its domestic foundations. In such a perspective, the Cold War had been sustained by America's mainstream culture, the 'culture of the middle class'. Counter-culture exponents advocated attacking this culture itself, the culture that had stressed themes such as America's domestic consensus, homogeneity, unity, or more generally national character that was unique. Instead of these notions, counter-culture advocates stressed America's ethnic diversity, separatism, or internal inconsistencies. These themes, combined with movements for civil rights, women's rights, and immigration law revision, developed as a powerful force for social transformation. It was because of such a movement that the opposition to the Vietnam war succeeded in gaining influence among significant segments of the population.

Such trends were echoed abroad. Student activism in Western Europe and Japan were among the clearest examples. Interestingly enough, just when Americans were becoming critical of their own society, their cultural influence, now taking the form of a counter-culture movement, spread world-wide. People abroad were deeply impressed with the way the American people challenged the existing social order and ideologies, and there developed a cross-national solidarity of reformers. While the military position of the United States suffered a setback in Southeast Asia, its prestige in this cultural sense may be said to have been enhanced. French intellectuals, for instance, who had tended to be ideologically anti-American, now began praising America's self-critical and self-regenerative ability.

Another challenge to the Cold War orthodoxy appeared in the Third World. Sometimes referred to as 'Third Worldism', the self-conscious assertiveness of non-Western and developing countries, which had arisen already during the 1950s, became much more conspicuous in the subsequent decade. The Third World now comprised more than one-half of the membership of the United Nations, which totalled 120 nations in 1964. While some of them focused on military strengthening, often engaging in local wars, most were intent on economic development, collectively as well as individually. For instance, in 1964, when the United Nations convened the first conference on trade and development (UNCTAD), the developing countries insisted that they should be given preferential treatment in the export of agricultural and semi-finished products. The increasing gaps between the value of trade of the advanced countries and of the rest of the world led to demands that the advanced countries should do something about it. In a way, this was politicizing an economic problem. The Third World's politicization became even clearer when many developing nations criticized the US war in Vietnam and became receptive to China's ideology of national liberation. Although not all of them subscribed to this ideology, and few embraced its more extreme variety after the onset of the Cultural Revolution in 1966, the spread of the national liberation ideology nevertheless provided another indication that international affairs were at a turning point.

How did Japan respond to these changes? How did the Japanese perceive the world of the 1960s? Fundamentally, they opted for the continuation of the policy of economic growth, combined with the security tie to the United States. But because this amounted to applying the policies of the 1950s to the changing world of the 1960s, questions were bound to be raised about the appropriateness of such a position.

Ikeda Hayato, who succeeded Kishi as prime minister in July 1960, spoke of maintaining a 'low posture' in national politics so as to calm domestic opinion after it had been inflamed during the anti-Kishi demonstrations. Ikeda practised the same policy externally as well, trying to avoid friction with other nations as much as possible and focusing on the economic well-being of the people. This was essentially carrying on the legacy of Yoshida's approach, but Ikeda was more confident of asserting Japan's economic role in the world. As he said at the end of 1962, when he returned from a European trip, 'the free world consists of three pillars: North America, Europe, and Japan'. Japan had much to learn from Europe, he said, especially the European countries' eagerness for promoting 'economic, not political', union. Their phenomenal economic growth was due to the people's 'enthusiasm and diligence' for building their nations, and Japan should do likewise. That was how the nation could best contribute to the international community. To carry out such an objective, in December 1960 the Ikeda cabinet announced an 'income-doubling plan', designed to double Japan's national income in ten years. The plan succeeded beyond expectation; Japan's nominal GNP increased from $33.3 billion in 1960 (about one-sixteenth of the US figure) to $203.4 billion in 1970 (about one-fifth). Even taking into consideration the inflation in the two countries, the real rate of growth in Japan was an amazing 10 per cent a year, in contrast to America's 3 per cent.

It should be noted that the international environment was quite favourable for such a policy. The 1960s were a decade of high economic growth globally, including the two superpowers, Western Europe, and the Third World. Thus Japan was able to increase its exports to all these countries, especially to the Third World which needed Japan's industrial machinery to undertake their own indus-trialization. Japan's exports increased from $8.5 billion in 1960 to $38.2 billion ten years later. In 1965 its trade recorded a surplus for the first time since the war. The fact that the yen's value was kept low, at the fixed rate of 360 yen to the dollar, made Japanese goods comparatively cheap in the world market. Trade surpluses resulted in increased amounts of foreign exchange (especially dollar) holdings, which in turn brought about a liberalization of trade and foreign exchange policies. Till then, Japan's liberalization had proceeded much more slowly than that of the European countries; protective tariffs and exchange controls had been instituted to increase exports and obtain dollars, but such controls could now be less and less justified. So Japan took initial steps towards liberalization. For instance, whereas in 1960 only 40 per cent of imports had been liberalized (that is, freed from various restrictions), by 1964 the ratio had been increased to 93 per cent. Such a step was necessary in order to join the group of advanced nations known as the 'article eight' members of the IMF. These were countries that had removed trade restrictions and engaged in unfettered mutual trade. That Japan was admitted as an 'article eight' nation indicated its complete reintegration into the international economic system. Likewise, at the 1963 GATT meeting, Japan was for the first time recognized as an 'article eleven' nation, that is, a country that did not restrict trade for reasons of balance of payments. That Japan had become one of the advanced industrial nations was made official in 1964, when it was admitted into the Organization for Economic Cooperation and Development (OECD).

Japanese trade with its Asian neighbours also grew. Trade with China had hit rock bottom after the crisis of 1958, but it began to show signs of recovery after 1960, and by 1963 the level of the bilateral trade regained that attained in 1957. One basic reason for this was that China now had greater need of Japanese products because of a deteriorating relationship with the Soviet Union. In the early 1960s thousands of Soviet technicians were called home, and Moscow demanded repayment for the loans it had extended to China in the 1950s. This was the time when China was reeling from the disastrous consequences of the Great Leap Forward, and its leaders were compelled to turn to Japan for obtaining items necessary for economic reconstruction and growth, such as iron and steel, chemical fertilizers, and various types of industrial machinery. The trade between the two countries amounted to $4.7 billion in 1965, which was only 2.8 per cent of total Japanese trade but constituted 12.4 per cent of China's. Japan was the biggest supplier of imported goods to China, accounting for about

14 per cent of China's total imports. Reflecting the growing economic interdependence, Japanese businessmen even signed contracts for establishing manufacturing plants in China. These were remarkable developments, considering the fact that throughout most of the 1960s Chinese foreign policy was stridently anti-US and anti-USSR. Beijing also was critical of Japan's policy of 'separation of politics and economics' and insisted that continued growth of the bilateral trade was possible only if this separation was ended and Japan stopped following the United States in a hostile policy towards China. Nevertheless, Chinese–Japanese trade grew even without a significant modification in their political relationship. After 1962 it was conducted in the framework of the so-called LT agreement, after the initials of Liao Chung-k'ai and Takasaki Tatsunosuke, who negotiated a new arrangement in which Japanese firms deemed 'friendly' towards Beijing would be permitted to engaged in the trade. These firms were to pledge that they would strive for normalization of Chinese–Japanese relations. This came close to politicizing the economic relationship, but in reality politics lagged far behind economics.

Another signifiant development in Japan's Asian affairs in the 1960s was the establishment of a formal diplomatic relationship with the government of South Korea. As seen earlier, negotiations for normalization had got nowhere in the 1950s, but things picked up momentum after the fall from power of Syngman Rhee in 1960. He had been adamantly opposed to making concessions to Japan, but his successors were more willing to settle for a compromise solution. In part this reflected economic considerations. Seoul had hitherto insisted on reparations payments by Japan, but now it was ready to substitute loans and grants for reparations. The economic consequences may have been the same, but Japan's reluctance to call the package a reparations payment indicated its interest in subordinating political issues to economic arrangements. The question of Japan's repayment for its colonial rule would not go away, however. In any event, the Japanese–Korean treaty of 1965 established diplomatic relations between the two countries. Japan offered Korea an outright grant of $300 million plus another $200 million as a loan, and in addition Tokyo promised private credits amounting at least to $300 million. Concerning the controversial question of Japanese property left behind in Korea, Japan would not seek any compensation in return for Koreans' giving up their claims over properties held in Japan. Late in the same year, Tokyo and Seoul signed a legal status agreement, whereby Koreans then in Japan – most of them had been forcibly brought to the country – and their offspring (the second-generation Koreans in Japan) would be given the status of permanent residents. The so-called 'right of permanent residency' was not the same thing as citizenship, but Korean residents in Japan would be differentiated from other foreigners who did not have this status. There was no precise definition of the right of permanent residence or of the status of future generations of Koreans in Japan; these problems would be left to future settlement. In the meantime, the mere fact that Japan and Korea established diplomatic relations was a momentous event in the history of postwar Japanese foreign affairs.

In Southeast Asia, too, Japan managed to complete all reparations payments. About $1 billion was paid to the Philippines, Indonesia, Burma, and Vietnam after a series of negotiations with individual countries. The reparations were combined with foreign aid so that economic ties between Japan and Southeast Asia grew even closer than earlier. It is true that the bulk of economic aid took the form of yen credits, which the recipients would use to import from Japan, thereby increasing Southeast Asia's economic dependence on Japan. But for Japan to extend even this type of economic assistance was something new, indicating that Japan was beginning to be aware of its obligations as an advanced economic power. Most other advanced countries spent about 1 per cent of their respective national incomes on aid, and Japan aspired to the same goal, although at this time it was impossible to realize it. In this connection, the Asian Development Bank which was established in 1966 offered an institutional setting for Japan's aid activities. The bank was founded on the basis of about $1.1 billion provided by the United States, Japan, and other countries, and aimed at assisting the economic development of Southeast Asian countries. The fact that the bank's headquarters was put in Manila, not Tokyo, may have reflected the lingering suspiciousness of Japan on the part of Asian countries, but its first president was Japanese, and many of his countrymen were to become quite active in the bank's affairs.

The Japanese government, in the meantime, continued the policy of keeping military expenditures low, relying on the US security treaty for national defence. Ikeda Hayato, who exemplified this approach, resigned on account of illness in December 1964 and was replaced by Satō Eisaku, but Satō did not significantly alter the policy. Japanese defence spending grew from 156.4 billion yen in 1960 to 569.5 yen ten years later, but the rate of increase was less than the rate of growth of the economy; Japan's national income in these years increased by more than four times. Such a relatively low level of military spending could be maintained because it was combined with the security arrangement with the United States. The Japan–US security treaty, which had aroused so much commotion in 1960, came to be accepted by the bulk of the Japanese people, although they did not give it their enthusiastic approval. According to a July 1968 survey by the *Mainichi* daily, 30 per cent of those polled supported the security treaty, 20 per cent opposed it, and 43 per cent 'could not make up their minds'. At the end of the year, *Mainichi* asked if people thought 'the United States will protect Japan in an emergency'. Only 24 per cent answered in the affirmative, while 51 per cent were not so sure. Still, only 12 per cent of those polled called for an immediate abrogation of the security treaty, while 31 per cent supported an automatic extension. Ambivalent as such attitudes were, they probably indicated general support for the security tie with the United States – but no major change in the treaty. Both Ikeda and Satō followed such views in continuing to turn to the United States for national security and, as a corollary, to maintain Japanese armament at a minimal level. The 1960 treaty, which was in effect for ten years, was quietly renewed in 1970.

While such a posture contributed one element of predictability and stability in international relations, it amounted to a continued posture of passivity on the part of Japan. At a time when world affairs were rapidly changing, Japan remained content under the US 'nuclear umbrella' and left major initiatives of strategic nature to the United States. Still, this did not mean that Japan was blindly following American policies and dictates. A good example was Tokyo's strong interest in seeking the retrocession of the Ryūkyū islands, usually known as Okinawa, the largest of the island group. It had remained under US military governance even after the 1952 peace treaty, although Okinawa's status as a part of Japan was never questioned. To pre-empt a public outcry for its reunification with the mainland, the Ikeda cabinet began informal talks with the United States, but it was Satō who showed an unusual interest in the issue. Convinced that without the islands' retrocession postwar settlements would not be complete, he visited Okinawa while in office, the first postwar prime minister to do so. He was given friendly encouragement by Edwin O. Reischauer, US ambassador in Japan during 1961–66 who also believed that the continuation of military government in Okinawa made the realization of 'partnership' between the two countries that much more difficult.

Although it was doubtful whether such a relationship was really possible, given their disparity in military power and international positions, at least Reischauer, Satō, and others were insistent that the partnership had to be built somewhere, and that Okinawa was a good place to start. Even so, negotiations for its reversion took several years. This was fundamentally because there was disagreement as to the status of Okinawa after its return to Japan. For both Japan and the United States assumed that US bases would continue to be operated in Okinawa. But should they be treated in the same way as those in Japan proper, that is, would the bases in Okinawa be covered by the stipulations of the 1960 security treaty, according to which the two countries were to engage in 'prior consultation' concerning US military operations and equipment? The United States at first insisted, and Satō agreed, that Okinawa should be exempted from the 'prior consultation' rule because it was the principal base of operation for the US forces in East Asia and also because these forces were (it was widely believed) equipped with nuclear weapons. At that time, US forces were engaged in the Vietnam war, and troops and planes stationed in Okinawa were mobilized for action in

Indochina. To ask for the return of the islands in such circumstances could potentially damage US–Japanese relations. But Japanese public opinion was adamant in insisting on the return of the Ryūkūs without making any special provisions for US bases there, and Satō ultimately came to the same view. Fortunately for him, the United States under President Richard M. Nixon was willing to accept such a stipulation, and Okinawa was duly rejoined to the mainland in 1972.

The flexible stance of the United States is all the more remarkable when one considers that Japanese attitudes towards the Vietnam war were not exactly those of a 'partner'. For instance, a *Yomiuri* poll of June 1966 found that 18 per cent of the respondents thought the United States was responsible 'for the failure to arrive at a peaceful solution of the Vietnam war', while 8 per cent blamed China, and 6 per cent each for North and South Vietnam. But as many as 62 per cent said they did not know the answer, indicating widespread public ignorance or indifference towards the war. There was nothing comparable to the 1960 mass movements, although some activists pursued a peace movement in coordination with the anti-war protests in the United States. At the same time, there was little support for US policy even on the part of the government in Tokyo. The 1968 edition of the Foreign Ministry's annual report (the so-called *Blue Book*) admitted as much, noting: 'Because of our constitutional restrictions and our people's pacifist sentiment, we have stood outside the Vietnam conflict in any military sense.' (The same document also mentioned that in 1968 Japan had passed the United States as Vietnam's number-one importer.) Clearly, Japan was not identifying itself with US strategy as far as Vietnam was concerned. One possible exception occurred in 1968 when the Satō cabinet decided to allow the nuclear-powered aircraft carrier *Enterprise* to enter the port of Sasebo for rest and recreation, despite the public's opposition on the grounds that the ship was equipped with nuclear arms. The coming of such a ship would be contrary to the 'three non-nuclear principles' which the government endorsed: that Japan would not manufacture, use, or introduce to its territory nuclear weapons. ' Instead of modifying the third principle to allow for the visit of the

Enterprise, the cabinet simply declared that it understood that the ship was not carrying nuclear weapons and could therefore allow its entry into a Japanese port. Despite such deviousness, Japan managed to maintain its adherence to the 'three non-nuclear principles' during the Vietnam war.

That was an important stance, for it meant that Japan would opt for the path of non-proliferation of nuclear arms, rather than that of nuclear armament, the choice the Chinese took in 1964. To that extent, Japan was siding with the United States and the Soviet Union against China. But such a stance proved of little value in anticipating a major shift in US policy towards China, culminating in the 1972 *rapprochement* between Washington and Beijing. Japan's non-nuclear strategy, in other words, made sense at one level, but it did not, in itself, contribute anything to changes in the global scene.

In other parts of Asia, however, Japan did take some significant steps. As already noted, it was able to normalize relations with Korea and to complete reparations payments with Southeast Asian countries. As if to mark a new chapter in Japan's Asian policy, Satō visited Korea and South Vietnam in 1967 in search for a non-military role for Japan. When, in August of that year, the Association of Southeast Asian Nations (ASEAN) was organized by Thailand, Indonesia, Malaysia, the Philippines, and Singapore, Japan was quick to view it as a stabilizing force and sought ways to cooperate with it. Likewise, Japan sent a delegate to participate in a ten-year anniversary celebration of the Bandung conference in 1965. It was as if Japan was on the threshold of an active Asian policy for the first time since the end of the war.

The problem was to define a basic approach, a philosophy, behind such an initiative. There was much discussion then about the ideological bases of Japanese foreign policy, but as yet little concrete emerged. Just to cite an example, in 1966 I wrote: 'The time seems to have come for Japan to establish a new ideological basis for its diplomacy. Japan's future should not be defined simply in terms of its own security or economic interests . . . but also of certain ideals that would connect Japan to the world so that the Japanese would dedicate themselves to achieving, besides their safety and prosperity, some sense of participation in world affairs.' Such a sentiment may have been widely shared in the mid-1960s, if one is to judge from numerous newspaper and magazine articles then. Kōsaka Masataka, of Kyoto University, for instance, published influential essays for *Chūōkōron*, such as 'A realist's view of peace' and 'Japan as a maritime nation'. He noted in these essays that the Japanese 'seem to have lost their sense of direction'. But the time had come, he said, to define anew national objectives as a guide to foreign policy. Kōsaka's advocacy of a maritime strategy was significant in that he took a global view, seeing the oceans as Japan's frontier, and suggested that the nation was in a unique position to work out its own agendas. Others, in contrast, asserted that Japan must pay more attention to Asia, especially China. Some went so far as to argue that the nation should reorient its diplomacy away from the Cold War to identifying itself with China's anti-imperialist, anti-hegemonist foreign policy. But the radicalism of the Cultural Revolution, which began in 1966, was too extreme even for Japan's China supporters, and they despaired of learning anything constructive, as against destructive, from Maoist ideology and diplomacy.

Prime Minister Satō, on his part, endeavoured to delineate the nature of Japanese foreign policy. In a speech at the National Press Club in Washington in November 1969, he referred to 'a new Pacific age'. He meant by the term the idea that Japan and the United States should closely cooperate in order 'to contribute to the peace and prosperity of Asia and the Pacific, and ultimately of the entire world'. There was little original in such a perspective; Satō still assumed that the security pact with the United States was at the core of Japanese foreign relations. But he added an important statement: 'Japan in the 1970s should try to offer non-military cooperation to Asian countries so that they, while representing divergent races, religions, and cultures, could enjoy freedom and independence and work with one another for their joint prosperity.' Japan was located in such a picture as the 'advanced industrial nation of Asia', with, therefore, a mission to share its wealth with others and to cooperate with them for a more peaceful regional order. While the idea of Japan's mission in Asia evoked memories of prewar pan-Asianism and the wartime slogan of coprosperity, neither of which had brought any welfare or peace to the region, Satō insisted that Japan's role this time was going to be non-military. In particular, he offered Japan's 'economic and technical aid' to nation-building efforts by Asians. In other words, militarily the nation would continue to rely on US power, but in economic and cultural spheres it would seek to play an 'active role' in Asia. Whether this would work, and whether other countries would accept such a role remained to be seen. It was obvious, in any event, that Japanese relations with the United States, too, were now being subtly redefined. As Satō said, the two countries that shared little racially or historically were about to launch 'an historical experiment to see if they can cooperate together for the creation of a new world order'. This may stand as an epitaph to Japanese diplomacy twenty-five years after the end of the war.

Chapter 12

DIPLOMACY IN THE AGE OF ECONOMIC CHAOS

Within a few months after Satō's above-quoted speech, unexpected developments occurred in international relations, confronting the nations of the world with fresh challenges in the 1970s.

To be sure, one thing did not change: the superpower status of the United States and the Soviet Union. They were still the only nuclear superpowers, and they added substantially to their stock of intercontinental ballistic missiles (ICBMs). America's ICBM warheads doubled in number in the 1970s, whereas the Soviet Union's quadrupled. At the same time, neither power augmented its existing arsenals of long-range bombers, missiles, or missile-loaded submarines. Moreover, in the 1970s both Washington and Moscow were willing to take some tentative steps towards limiting nuclear armament. Already in the preceding decade, they had come to the conclusion that a nuclear war against each other had become unthinkable, and they had supported restrictions on nuclear testing and called for non-proliferation of nuclear weapons. But they were now going a step further, reasoning that any additional nuclear build-up made no sense at all. They could now agree to limit further build-ups, in effect freezing the nuclear status quo. The historic agreement of 1972 to limit strategic arms was designed to preserve 'parity' in the number of ICBMs and SLBMs (submarined-launched ballistic missiles) the two powers possessed. Because prior to the 1970s the United States had held the most powerful nuclear arsenal, such an agreement implied that this position was undergoing change. The relative decline in the military position of the United States was also reflected in its conventional forces and defence budgets. In the late 1960s, because of the war in Vietnam, the nation maintained a force totalling some 3.5 million, which was more than the armed forces of the Soviet Union. But during the 1970s, US military strength was reduced to 2 million, while the Soviet force continued to be increased till it was twice as large as the US armed force. As if to symbolize this contrast, while US forces were withdrawn from Vietnam, Soviet troops invaded Afghanistan. In defence spending, too, the United States had expended more in the 1960s than the Soviet Union, but the situation was reversed in the 1970s, so that by the end of the decade the Soviet Union was spending 50 per cent more than the United States on defence.

The picture was part of a major reorientation in US world strategy, as President Nixon and his national security adviser, Henry Kissinger (secretary of state after 1973), sought to develop a global balance of power in which not just the two nuclear giants but China and the European nations would play a part. Kissinger's dramatic trip to China in the summer of 1971, followed by Nixon's visit to Beijing and Shanghai (where he and Chou En-lai signed an important joint communiqué, normalizing relations between the two countries), were attempts at adding China to the world geopolitical picture. They were derived from the realization that the strategy of dealing with both the Soviet Union and China as adversaries was no longer tenable, and that it would make sense to bring China into the regional balance. To do so, of course, would nullify the hitherto fundamental rationale of the Vietnam war, namely to contain mainland China. So the 1972 Nixon trip to China had a logical consequence in the 1975 withdrawal of all US forces from Vietnam. For the Shanghai communiqué clearly stated that neither China nor the United States would seek hegemony in the Asia–Pacific region; it implied that the latter would cease to engage in the kind of unilateral military action that it had pursued in Southeast Asia.

In Europe, too, there were trends towards relaxing the rigid pattern of confrontation between the members of NATO and the Warsaw Pact. In 1971 the superpowers recognized the two Germanies, enabling them both to join the United Nations. Washington and Moscow also agreed to respect the status quo on the status of Berlin, putting an end to the long-standing contention over this issue. The establishment of the Conference on Security and Co-operation in Europe (CSCE) in 1972 was a landmark, bringing together for the first time the NATO and Warsaw Pact nations. The setting provided a forum where members of the two Cold War camps could establish contact. At the Helsinki meeting of CSCE in 1975, these nations agreed to work for stabilization in Europe through reduction of tactical nuclear weapons as well as of conventional arms.

All such moves indicated a willingness on the part of the United States, the Soviet Union, China, and other nations to deflect the world from confrontation and tensions and to cooperate for a more stable international order. This state of affairs was called a 'detente'. To be sure, such willingness was severely tested at the end of the decade when Soviet forces invaded and occupied Afghanistan and the United States retaliated by boycotting the 1980 Moscow Olympics. But even these crises did not put an end to the detente, as shown by the fact that negotiations went on between Washington and Moscow concerning further restrictions on nuclear weapons. Moreover, China definitely re-entered the international arena when it established diplomatic relations with Japan in 1972 and the United States in 1979. China's invasion of Vietnam in February 1979, like the Soviet action in Afghanistan, was contrary to the trend towards re-stabilization, but even so China's leadership after the conclusion of the Cultural Revolution (in 1976) was clearly more desirous of stability than of revolutionary upheaval in its foreign affairs.

These developments gave rise to the term 'polycentrism' or 'multipolarity', suggesting that world geopolitical power was no longer centred on the two nuclear giants. At this time, however, power was not quite diffused. It would be more correct to say that China was emerging as a potential third superpower. It was avidly promoting 'four modernizations', of which the most important was the modernization of armed forces, and the country's defence expenditures were next only to those of the two super-powers. Some sort of balance among the three was a possibility. This was what Kissinger had in mind when he spoke of a 'new structure of peace'. It should be noted, however, that the Chinese leadership continued to vow that China would never become a military superpower. As Teng Hsiao-p'ing (Deng Xiaoping) said at the United Nations in 1974, China viewed itself as a member of the Third World, never a superpower. At this time it was difficult to tell whether this, or Kissinger's, perception was more appropriate.

If global geopolitics appeared to be entering a period of redefinition and restabilization, in sharp contrast was the world economy, for which the decade of the 1970s was one of confusion, even of chaos. First of all, the Bretton Woods system, based on the role of the dollar as the international medium of exchange, could no longer be sustained when the American currency began to weaken because of inflation and fiscal deficits. To make matters worse, the United States recorded trade deficits from 1973 onwards, for the first time since 1894, owing to the rising cost of American goods in the world market as well as steady increases in imports from abroad. Reflecting these developments, the relative value of the dollar against other currencies (such as the German mark, the French franc, and the yen) fell, with the result that these countries held huge amounts of dollars. If they were to exchange them for gold, as was practised under the Bretton Woods system, large amounts of gold would be shipped out of the United States, further destabilizing financial conditions. To cope with the situation, President Nixon banned gold payments for dollars, thus in effect admitting that the US currency had lost the value it had maintained since the end of the war. The existing rates of exchange with other currencies, which had hitherto been more or less stable, could no longer be maintained, and all efforts to work out new rates failed. After 1973 exchange rates among different currencies were allowed to 'float', resulting in a substantial fall in the value of the dollar *vis-à-vis* some other currencies. Also in 1971, the US government put a temporary 10 per cent surcharge on all imports in order to improve the nation's balance of trade. This was another indication that the unquestioned supremacy of the United States as the main trading nation was eroding. More seriously, such a measure undermined the open international trading system so laboriously worked out under GATT.

If these developments showed a relative decline of US economic power and, in contrast, the growing economic might of Western Europe and Japan, all these countries were shaken by the 'oil shock' of 1973–74, when the Organization of Petroleum Exporting Countries (OPEC) curtailed the production of petroleum and increased the price of crude oil that was sold through international cartels from $4 a barrel to $11. This challenge by the Third World was devastating for the advanced nations, causing inflation, trade deficits, and even zero or minus rates of growth. The world economy that had kept expanding throughout most of the 1950s and the 1960s now entered the period of 'stagflation', combining economic stagnation and inflation. Rising prices discouraged consumption and caused unemployment. Workers' real incomes declined. When OPEC carried out a second price increase in 1979, it seemed as if the world economy would never again be the same. Some feared a reversion to the 1930s, in which a global economic crisis had provided the setting for the rise of totalitarianism and paved the road for aggression and war.

Fortunately, however, this time the advanced nations were determined never to go back to the 1930s. Six of them (the United States, Britain, France, West Germany, Italy, and Japan) held a summit conference in Rambouillet, outside of Paris, in 1975 to reaffirm their commitment for solving the economic crisis through cooperation. They pledged to work for exchange stability and free trade. Although little specific came of the meeting, the mere fact that the leaders of the economic powers met was important (no such gathering had taken place during 1933–44). The 'economic summit' was to be held every year and in time include the leaders of Canada and the European Community (later European Union). Another important contrast to the 1930s was the fact that this time world trade did not decline but, on the contrary, continued to increase. The value of total world trade (outside of Soviet-bloc countries) was some $569.2 billion in 1970, which increased to $3,691.8 billion by 1980. Of course, inflation and the diminished value of the dollar must be taken into consideration, but even so the volume of trade steadily increased throughout the decade. It is interesting to note that for most advanced countries, the proportion of trade as a percentage of GDP (gross domestic product) increased between the 1960s and the 1970s: for the United States from 10 to 15 per cent, for Britain from 42 to 54 per cent, for West Germany from 37 to 45 per cent, and for France from 28 to 39 per cent. In other words, for all these countries (including Japan, as will be noted), trade was, if anything, more important than ever. To promote trade expansion, they judged that they must maintain a framework of international cooperation.

The situation in the rest of the world was more complicated. One of the significant developments in the 1970s was that the Third World, which had been identified as a group of underdeveloped countries, began to be split into several groups, some far richer than others. Particularly notable was the wealth of the oil-exporting nations in the Middle East and elsewhere, whose per capita income grew from $2,054 in 1970 to $7,390 ten years later. (The average per capita income of the advanced nations grew from $6,098 to $10,660 in the same decade.) Their trade showed significant surpluses due to the increasing price of oil, and some countries, such as Saudi Arabia and Kuwait, came to hold large quantities of foreign exchange. In sharp contrast were other Third World nations, whose average GNP was only $459 in 1970 and $850 in 1980. Some 54 per cent of the world's population belonged to this category, and they were accumulating trade deficits as well as balance of payments deficits. Still, some of them, notably in Asia (such as Taiwan and South Korea), were making successful attempts to adjust to the rising costs of imported oil and paving the way for their spectacular growth in the 1980s.

Thus, the Third World as a term became less and less meaningful. At the same time, many Third World countries became more nationalistic than ever, in economic and military affairs. They began insisting on their sovereign rights over territorial coastlines and continental shelves, asserting their sovereignty over 200 miles of water, going much beyond the traditional limit of 30 miles. (The advanced countries, too, followed suit.) Militarily, many Third World countries built up arms even when their economies were suffering from the world-wide recession and oil-induced inflation. Huge quantities of arms were purchased from the advanced countries, indicating that the export of weapons to underdeveloped countries became an important part of the advanced countries' foreign trade. The United States, for instance, even while it reduced its military spending, increased weapons shipments abroad. All these developments were clearly introducing elements of uncertainty in world affairs.

Interestingly enough, such uncertainty may have provided an impetus for the search for moral and religious certitude that characterized political and cultural developments of the 1970s. Ideological certainty was clearly an objective sought by both the Catholic church and Islam. Within both, movements grew in such a way as to challenge existing political authority. Typical were Ayatollah Khomeini's Islamic fundamentalism in Iran and the 'salvation theology' in Mexico and other American states. Both had mass following and reflected a reaction against the established forces in national and international affairs. In the United States, too, there was a notable increase in the influence of revivalism and evangelicalism, movements that appealed to the emotions and moral senses of the people. The 'moral majority' movement in the southern states was one prominent instance. Similar in nature, though different in content, were movements for democracy that spread in Spain, Portugal, Poland, and later in other countries. They, too, shook the foundations of the national systems of power, opposing them by asserting the rights of civil (or civic) society.

International affairs could not but reflect these trends. President James E. Carter's human rights diplomacy was, in a way, a response to the search for a new ideological basis of foreign policy in a period of rapid change and confusion. Of course, human rights was an old concept and had been asserted time and again, for instance in Franklin D. Roosevelt's 'four freedoms' speech or UNESCO's universal declaration of human rights. But world affairs since the war had not promoted these rights as a primary objective but had instead been characterized by military and security affairs. More recently, economic issues had become critical, but ideologically, the world had not gone much beyond the Cold War ideas or Third World nationalism, neither of which had provided a universalistic basis for international affairs.

In the 1970s, however, there were attempts at developing

concepts and attitudes that were more transnational and spoke to the needs and aspirations of people everywhere. The 1975 Helsinki gathering of CSCE was a landmark in this regard; thirty-five countries from both camps in the Cold War came together and agreed to cooperate in promoting human rights and the exchange of people and information. Of course, there were different interpretations of what constituted human rights, and there was no agreement as to how their violation in one country was to be dealt with by others. Andrei Sakharov, the prominent Soviet scientist, criticized the West for not putting more pressure on the socialist-bloc nations to achieve greater openness. But at least it was significant that, for the first time since the early postwar years, the Soviet Union joined the United States in support of universalistic principles. Although human-rights diplomacy was never consistently pursued even by the United States – for instance, it continued to provide military assistance to Pakistan despite that country's suppression of democratic movements – it was important that, alongside national security and trade, democratization came to be viewed as a central part of the foreign affairs not just of the United States but of other countries as well. To the extent that human rights, if promoted without restriction, could challenge the governmental authority of most existing states, this phenomenon was suggestive of a significant new factor in world affairs, the growth of the sense of power on the part of people across national boundaries and, as a corollary, the erosion of the power of the state.

How did Japan respond to these new currents? It is difficult to say that it was ready to define a new role in international affairs. In military affairs, it showed little initiative but, as in the past, rather passively followed the American lead. In the security sphere, such passivity was graphically demonstrated when the United States, right after renewing the Japanese security treaty in 1970, reversed its policy towards China without prior consultation with Japan, which had dutifully followed the US policy of not recognizing the Beijing regime or supporting its replacement of Taipei in the United Nations as the government of China. All of a sudden, however, the Japanese felt 'shocked' by what they came to call the 'power game': they felt confused about the ways in which the big powers seemed to play their games. If the United States, Japan's major (and perhaps only) ally, could behave thus, how would the nation ever be able to find a secure basis for its conduct of foreign affairs? They had no immediate answer, but they concluded that the only choice they had was, once again, to follow the United States. Hardly had they recovered from the 'shock' than they began making plans for a *rapprochement* with the People's Republic of China. Thus seven months after Nixon visited China (in February 1972), Prime Minister Tanaka Kakuei followed suit. The Japanese–Chinese communiqué of 29 September, establishing diplomatic relations between the two nations, sounded very similar to the US–China Shanghai communiqué. Both included the identical language about opposing any country's seeking to establish hegemony in the Asia–Pacific region. Sensing that this expression was aimed at the Soviet Union, Tanaka was reluctant to include it in the joint statement, but in the end he accepted it, thereby ensuring that among Japan, China, and the United States there would be some strategic common ground for the first time since the war.

For Japan this meant a significant transformation of its foreign affairs. In addition to the US security connection, now the new ties with China were seen as a foundation-stone of the Asia–Pacific regional order. China, in other words, was no longer seen as existing outside the US–Japanese security system but as being compatible with it. The Chinese leaders clearly recognized the change and were willing to show their 'understanding' for the security pact. Although the Chinese were motivated primarily by their concern with Soviet power, for the Japanese the new departure was welcome since they no longer had to choose between the United States and China.

It is to be noted, however, that all these changes were brought about from the outside, through the US initiative and China's reformulation of its foreign policy, not through Japan's own re-examination of its strategic priorities. This becomes all the clearer when it is noted that throughout the 1970s there was little change in Japan's defence policy. The nation was still committed to eschewing a military role in international affairs, in a sense continuing to behave non-geopolitically in a changing world. This stance may have been confirmed by the very geopolitical phenomenon of the US–PRC *rapprochement*, for without it Japan might have been impelled to reconsider its passive defence policy in response to the relative decline of US military power. President Nixon's Guam doctrine, implying that Asians must contribute more to their own security, might have resulted in a more assertive military role by Japan. But such a choice did not have to be made now that the possibility of conflict between the United States and China receded. Thus the Washington–Beijing normalization had the effect of enabling Japan to continue the low military posture it had assumed since the 1950s.

A good example of this was the 1976 'Outline of Defence Plans', which the cabinet adopted in 1976. This was the first official statement of defence policy since the 1957 document, 'Basic Guidelines for National Defence', and reflected the need to redefine Japanese security policy in view of the rapid changes in international affairs. But the content of the 1976 document mostly reiterated the existing positions, as seen in the key statement:

> The basis of our defence policy is to prevent an attack on the nation through maintaining an appropriate level of defence capabilities, developing a system for deploying them most effectively, maintaining the integrity of the security arrangement with the United States, making necessary adjustments so as to implement smoothly this arrangement, and organizing our defence system so as to respond to any type of invasion.

The 'Outline' pointed out that 'a certain equlibrium has developed among the United States, the Soviet Union, and China', but that at the same time 'tensions in the Korean peninsula have persisted, and many neighbouring countries are augmenting their military forces'. Still, Japan was not about to alter its existing defence policy. To be sure, Japanese military spending grew throughout the 1970s, quadrupling between 1970 and 1980 in yen figures, but its proportion in annual governmental outlays decreased from 7.24 per cent to 5.24 per cent in the decade. As a percentage of GNP, Japanese defence expenditures never exceeded 1 per cent, a fact that was made into an official guideline by the cabinet of Prime Minister Miki Takeo in 1975. Even so, Japanese defence spending in 1978 (about $10 billion) was already the ninth largest in the world. This was still lower than China's estimated defence budget, but three time as large as South Korea's. Still, there was no new strategic doctrine behind such increases, and the '1 per cent' guideline suggested that there would be no drastic departure in the nation's security policy.

Japanese policy was somewhat more assertive with regard to international economic issues, ranging from the dollar crisis of 1971 to the oil shocks of 1973 and 1979. Fundamentally, Japanese policy-makers were anxious to maintain cooperation with other nations so as to prevent a return to the 1930s-type situation of excessive economic nationalism. Time and again, Tokyo's leaders expressed their continued commitment to an open, multilateral system of economic transactions. For instance, in the 1973 *Blue Book*, the Foreign Ministry asserted that Japan had a special obligation as one of the economic powers to affirm the vitality of GATT, IMF, and other arrangements. This could best be done by 'improving our economic system so as to promote openness and to contribute positively to the construction of a new world economic order'. Japan could thrive only when the whole world was prosperous and could undertake growth only through international cooperation.

Even the authors of the *Blue Book* recognized, however, that the Japanese economy had not been exactly open. Barriers to multilateral trade had existed, but such measures had not given rise to serious disputes with other countries, including the United States which had acquiesced in them in the belief that an economically developed Japan was a positive force for international stability. Now, however, such exceptionalism was no longer tenable when Japanese trade (in 1970) amounted to 6 per cent of the world's total, making it the fifth largest trading nation after the United States, West Germany, Britain, and France. These countries were beginning to be alarmed over the quick pace of Japan's trade expansion. The *Blue Book* pointed out that trade friction with such countries was possible if Japan gave the impression of disrupting the normal working of foreign markets, which could indeed be the case because of the export-oriented industrial policy that had promoted fiscal and monetary measures so as to focus available resources on plant investment.

As if to prove the accuracy of such predictions, serious trade friction developed with other countries, particularly the United States. At first, to be sure, Japanese exports did not grow because of the Nixon and oil shocks; the upward revaluation of the yen *vis-à-vis* the dollar made Japanese goods more expensive, while the steep rise in the price of crude oil boosted the value of imports into Japan. Inflation at home invited the increased importation of other commodities as well, so that for a while after 1974 Japan recorded trade deficits. It was not until 1982 that Japanese trade began consistently showing export surpluses. Still, combining exports and imports, total Japanese trade increased seven-fold during the 1970s, an amazing fact even though commodity prices increased by 150 per cent during the decade. Japan's share in world trade reached 8 per cent by 1980. It was this type of rapid trade expansion that heightened tensions in Japanese economic relations with the United States and other countries. As early as October 1977, the *Bungei shunjū* monthly published a special issue entitled 'The Japanese-American economic war'. By then, America's trade deficits had begun to exceed $10 billion, a large portion of it attributable to the unfavourable balance of trade with Japan. For instance, in 1977, US trade deficits amounted to $29.1 billion, of which $8.0 billion, or 28 per cent, were in trade with Japan. Such a huge import surplus from Japan was partly due to the fact that Japan, in order to pay for higher-priced imported petroleum, sharply increased its export of cars and electronics (colour television sets, tape-recorders, etc.) to the United States. Till the late 1960s, the most conspicuous Japanese goods imported to the United States had been textiles and steel, which had not seemed threatening to American workers and their Congressional representatives. Now, however, Japan was selling those items, like cars and colour television, which had long been viewed as America's particularly strong specialities. 'The trade war', *Bungei shunjū* writers noted, 'really amounts to competition for jobs.' American workers for the first time came to feel alarmed about their jobs as a result of Japanese imports. Under the circumstances, the United States began viewing Japan as a major competitor.

Japan–US relations from then on came to be defined as much by trade as by security issues. Although the United States continued to uphold its security pacts with Japan and other allies, Kissinger publicly declared that such strategic cooperation was possible 'only when there is economic cooperation'. This was new language, the language of 'cooperative competition', a phrase often used in the United States then.

Japan, whose value of trade as a portion of the GDP increased from 20 per cent in 1970 to 30 per cent in 1980, could not ignore these new developments. Fearing US retaliation unless something were done, the government in Tokyo, under the guidance of the Ministry of International Trade and Industry (MITI), agreed to institute export restrictions. Starting with textiles, other goods, ranging from steel to colour television, were placed under numerical ceilings, either by Japan voluntarily or through a 'market maintenance' agreement with the United States. In addition, MITI sought to counter charges of 'dumping' by exhorting Japanese exporters to avoid cutting export prices.

As Japanese exports to the United States kept on growing in the second half of the 1970s despite such efforts, the Japanese government started to remove barriers to foreign imports. In 1970, some 90 imported items had been placed under quotas, a practice that had been assailed as a 'non-tariff barrier'. Tokyo reduced this number to only 27 by 1980. Of these, as many as 22 were agricultural products, about whose protection from foreign competition the Japanese government was adamant. Thus, despite the fact that the average import duty in Japan was only 2.5 per cent, there remained the image of the Japanese market as still very closed. Rice, beef, and citrus fruits, all of which were under quotas, came to symbolize this closed nature of the Japanese economy. Nevertheless, Tokyo was at least willing to accept the principle of trade liberalization. The government recognized that the nation, as an economic power, could no longer maintain non-tariff barriers or accumulate huge trade surpluses. A trade mission was sent to the United States to facilitate American exports to Japan. A new cabinet position of minister for external economic affairs was established in order to 'maintain free trade'. Although the position was not long maintained, these efforts were calculated to show the seriousness with which the Japanese were taking the trade problem. In 1978, Prime Minister Fukuda Takeo asserted in Washington that 'the Japanese market now is as open as the American market'. But Americans found it hard to believe such a situation existed, for Japanese trade with the United States continued to show export surpluses, in ever greater amounts.

Interestingly enough, the trade difficulties were often linked to cultural differences. Fukuda himself argued, when he defended Japan's agricultural protectionism, that 'Japan needs farmers to preserve a healthy society, and we do not want to impoverish them further' through liberalization of agricultural imports. This was arguing from a socio-cultural perspective. Others, inside and outside the country, noted that Japan's complicated distribution system or peculiar inter-business structures such as *keiretsu* (a system of mutual dependence among firms) and *dangō* (consultation prior to putting in bids) were hindering a smooth functioning of trade relations. These, too, were cultural phenomena broadly defined, and thus international economic issues tended to be broadened to include cultural ones.

As suggested earlier, the attention paid to cultural phenomena was an important aspect of international relations of the 1970s. While few Japanese put culture at the basis of their foreign affairs, there was realization that alongside security and economic questions, the nation should be thinking of a cultural role to play in the world. A good example was the establishment of the Japan Foundation in 1972. It was visualized as the successor to Kokusai Bunka Shinkōkai which had been organized in 1934 to promote cultural exchanges. The Japan Foundation at its inception was a modest operation, with the initial public funding of only 5 billion yen. It was placed under the supervision of the foreign minister, indicating that cultural exchange programmes were being viewed as an important feature of Japanese diplomacy. In 1973, when Prime Minister Tanaka visited the United States, he donated $1 million each to ten leading American universities to promote their Japanese studies programmes. Such grants reflected the thought that it was of vital importance for Japan–US relations to assist in the growth of the number of individuals knowledgeable about each other's country.

Similar, though more modest, programmes were launched in Western Europe and Southeast Asia. Thus in the summer of 1977, when Prime Minister Fukuda toured Southeast Asian countries, he stressed the importance of cultural interchange among them and between those nations and Japan. Keenly aware that in 1974, when Tanaka visited the region, he had been met with massive anti-Japanese demonstrations, Fukuda took pains to stress the vital necessity of establishing 'heart-to-heart contact' among Asians. In Asia, he said, it was crucial to try to 'understand one another's hearts and minds', besides pursuing security and economic relations. Here, too, was visible evidence of the importance of culture in foreign affairs. Likewise, Ōhira Masayoshi, who became prime minister at the end of the decade, repeatedly pointed out that 'the age of culture' had arrived; the world was moving away from 'the economic-centric age to an age which emphasizes culture', he asserted. That being the case, Japan must view the whole world as one community and define its roles and responsibilities accordingly. In order to do so, the nation must promote cultural 'internationalization' and train 'inter- nationally-oriented individuals'. Ōhira was correctly reading one key trend in world affairs at that time and was eager to fit Japan into it.

It was easy to speak of internationalization, but far more difficult to practise it. Ōhira's own ideas about this were lacking in specifics. For instance, he said that Japan had successfully undertaken 'Western-style modernization' and as a consequence tended to neglect 'our own unique spiritual culture'. Neither such an idea nor the assertion that Japan must make it a national objective 'to create a grand culture' went much beyond the slogans of the 1930s. It was far from clear what kind of culture Japan was to 'create', or how. For instance, in 1980 Japan followed the United States in boycotting the Moscow Olympics, but the reasons were geopolitical. It was not at all clear how such a decision might affect Japan's pursuit of cultural exchanges (which naturally included sports). On the other hand, there was an active promotion of cultural exchanges with China. In 1979, Prime Minister Ōhira told his Beijing audience that 'the most important aspect of international relations is the firm trust that connects the hearts and minds of peoples'.

Because, he added, the two countries 'have had two thousand years of friendly mutual visitations and cultural interactions', this history should enable them to construct an amicable relationship that went beyond temporary moods or economic interests. As if to respond to such an appeal, already in 1980 15,000 Chinese visited Japan, and 60,000 Japanese went to China. Most of them were students and scholars, thus playing an important role in scholarly communication between the two nations.

It is true that such communication did not make a visible impact on other aspects of Chinese or Japanese policies. For instance, China's one-party dictatorship was not affected at all by these exchanges, nor was its war with Vietnam. On Japan's side, it did not emulate the United States in promoting a human rights diplomacy as an aspect of cultural exchange programmes. Nevertheless, it may be said that in the 1970s Japan's leaders were becoming self-conscious, perhaps for the first time since the war, about Japan's position and role in the international community. According to Fukuda, Japan chose to preserve its 'three non-nuclear principles' even though it had 'economic and technological capabilities to manufacture nuclear weapons'. This was because, he said, the Japanese had decided not to become a military power. Ōhira, on his part, remarked that Japan must make a commitment 'for promoting mutual understanding in the global community'. In order to do so, it was important to develop a 'comprehensive national security system' that embraced Japan's 'military, economic, diplomatic, and creative cultural forces'. All these expressions were self-conscious responses to the changing world environment.

Chapter 13

THE POST-COLD WAR
WORLD

The 1980s began unpromisingly. In the wake of the Soviet
invasion of Afghanistan, it seemed as if the US–USSR
detente were being replaced by a renewed Cold War.
President Ronald Reagan, concerned over the gaps in the
two superpowers' defence budgets and conventional
weapons, sought to augment American military power.
United States defence spending, which comprised 22.7 per
cent of governmental outlays in 1980, increased to 28.1 per
cent by 1987. The United States used force in Grenada
(1983) and in Libya (1986). Anti-ballistic missiles (ABM),
which had been banned by SALT II – this agreement,
however, had not been ratified – were developed once
again, and a Strategic Defence Initiative (SDI), or the so-
called Star Wars, began being contemplated. The Soviet
Union opposed SDI, not having sufficient economic
resources to develop its own version of this, but it placed
tactical nuclear missiles (SS20s) in Europe. The West, in
turn, responded by putting in Pershing-II missiles. In this
way, the gravity of the military confrontation between the
two camps increased for the first time since the late 1960s.
Perhaps because of this very gravity, peace movements
picked up momentum both in the United States and in
Europe.

In retrospect, these moments of renewed crisis proved to
be short-lived. Within a few years, the world took dramatic
steps to ease tensions and indeed to end the Cold War
confrontation. In 1987 President Reagan and Mikhail
Gorbachev, general secretary of the USSR Communist party,
signed an INF agreement, aiming at abolishing

intermediate-range nuclear forces, resulting in the withdrawal from Europe of SS20s and Pershing-II missiles. Reagan and Gorbachev visited each other's country, CSCE meetings were resumed, and negotiations for reducing strategic nuclear weapons (START) began. In 1989 Soviet troops withdrew from Afghanistan, and talks began for reducing conventional forces in Europe. The Soviet Union and China, on their part, normalized their relations, putting an end to twenty years of animosity. Within the countries of Europe, there were even more dramatic developments, with drastic political changes taking place in the Soviet Union, Poland, Hungary, Czechoslovakia, Romania, and elsewhere. These countries abandoned their anti-Western, anti-US stances and approached the West economically and culturally. The Berlin wall was torn down, leading to the reunification of Germany. The fact that both the United States and the Soviet Union accepted a reunified Germany demonstrated that not only the Cold War but the Second World War, too, had finally ended.

This was only the most dramatic series of events. The 1980s witnessed other, equally significant developments. Economically, the decade was in sharp contrast to the 1970s in recording impressive growth rates throughout the world, especially in Asia. There were several reasons for this. For one thing, the United States finally came out of several years of 'stagflation', thanks to the Reagan administration's tax cuts and fiscal retrenchment, designed to stimulate the economy without inflation. The economy and the government required, and attracted, huge amounts of foreign capital. These developments in turn led to increased domestic consumption and foreign imports. Large portions of these imports came from Asian countries, contributing to the spectacular growth of many of their economies. Furthermore, the European nations took collective steps towards integration, creating a source of tremendous economic power. Finally, all nations succeeded in reducing energy consumption, thus decreasing their demand for, and bringing down the price of, petroleum. These factors combined to bring about an era of relative economic expansion and prosperity.

Some countries, to be sure, did not partake of this prosperity. The Soviet Union and Eastern Europe, for instance, recorded chronic trade deficits, as their production did not keep pace with demand, leading to increases in imports. Mexico, Brazil, the Philippines, and several other countries accumulated huge debts and proved unable to repay them. Earlier, they might have appealed to the United States for help, but it too was turning into a net debtor nation for the first time since the First World War. Governmental debts in 1987 amounted to $2,345,600 million, and fiscal deficits to $149,700 million. American trade for that year showed an import surplus of $160,200 million, the highest trade deficit in the nation's history. Still, there was no sense of alarm, since American deficits could be financed by the continued importation of European and Japanese funds. In other words, for Europe and Japan, the United States was a very attractive market for investment and loans. This could be seen in the fact that, even after the dollar was drastically devalued against the mark and the yen in 1985, it continued to be the most widely accepted international currency. It was in the interest of other countries to support the dollar's position, for no nation was ready to replace the United States as the economic superpower.

At the same time, the worsening economic conditions among the East-bloc nations could be credited with bringing about major changes in their foreign and domestic affairs. Gorbachev was quick to establish the connection; for him, Soviet economic reconstruction would be impossible so long as the arms race with the United States continued. The time had come, he recognized, to end the arms race, begin close cooperation with the Western powers, and to liberalize systems of production and distribution. He knew that such reorientation implied allowing political diversity and intellectual freedom at home; he even spoke of democracy and the 'four freedoms'. Without fundamental political reforms, he was convinced, there could be no economic rebuilding for the Soviet Union. This interconnectedness between economic prosperity and political reform, including disarmament, was a characteristic aspect of the international affairs of the 1980s. It was in a way reminiscent of a similar equation in the 1920s, or of the peace ideas of the 1940s, but in the 1980s it seemed as if those earlier visions might be finally coming close to realization.

In a sense the world was becoming more than ever Americanized. American ideals symbolized by the 'four freedoms' were spreading all over the world. Not just in the Soviet Union and Eastern Europe, but also in China, South Korea, the Philippines, and elsewhere waves of democratization were enveloping people and leaders alike. These political and ideological forces were defining a new pattern of international relations. To the extent that this pattern reflected American ideals and visions, it meant the reaffirmation of American ideological dominance forty years after the inception of the Cold War. It should be recalled that even in the United States visions of freedom and democracy had tended to be subordinated to geopolitical considerations during the height of the Cold War. The fact that the world was becoming Americanized meant, then, that for the first time since the war those ideals and visions were accepted by the world as universal ideals and shared dreams, not as Cold War ideologies. It is suggestive that precisely when America's relative military and economic power began to decline, its ideals became more universally influential than ever before.

Another way of looking at this phenomenon is to note the increasing porousness of nations. Just as American ideas were spreading to other countries, thereby Americanizing them, other countries' people and goods were entering the United States in larger quantities than ever before. American society was beginning to look like a microcosm of the world. There even grew 'Third World' problems in American cities, characterized by poverty, unemployment, or drug abuse. Even as the world was becoming Americanized, America was becoming globalized.

One can note the phenomenon of borderlessness in other instances. For example, both religious movements (by the Catholic church, Islam, and others) and ethnic activities across national boundaries challenged the existing system of international relations built upon sovereign states by stressing cross-national forces. Even within existing states, civil society (various organizations and individuals outside the government apparatus) increased its influence over state authority, and some components of the civil societies of various nations developed cross-national ties. The growth of non-governmental organizations (NGOs) in the 1980s reinforced this tendency. Some were radically opposed to the existing system of international affairs. Greenpeace, for instance, asserted their autonomy and their right to challenge any nation that harmed the natural environment. Other environmental groups were less radical, but they all sought to establish connections among forces in various countries committed to the protection of the natural habitat, ranging from rain forests and rivers to the ozone layer. This global concern with the environment suggested that international relations as traditionally understood, namely military and economic affairs among sovereign states, were in urgent need of redefinition. Issues that cut across national boundaries and that went beyond security or trade were gaining in importance. As best exemplified in the Chernobyl nuclear catastrophe, no one country could solve an environmental problem by itself. Likewise, other issues like the drug traffic or the spread of AIDS could only be dealt with internationally. In a sense, the very survival of humanity now hinged on cross-national cooperation. In such a situation, the role of sovereign states, which had constituted the foundation of modern international affairs, could not but become more and more limited.

Finally, another major development of the 1980s was the growth of regionalism, or the movement for establishing regional communities of nations. This, too, was another aspect of the same phenomenon, the transformation of traditional patterns of international relations. The most remarkable example of this, of course, was Europe, where its component nations aimed at removing their national boundaries by 1992 so that citizens of all those countries would be free to live and work where they pleased. Ultimately, there was the expectation that Eastern European countries, too, would become part of the picture. The big question in the decade was whether other regions of the world might do likewise. Already the United States and Canada were entering into a free trade agreement, and some Asian and Pacific nations were promoting the idea of an Asian–Pacific regional community. Only in Africa and the Middle East, there was as yet little visible evidence of such a development. In any event, here was another sign of the passing of familiar frameworks of international affairs.

Already in the 1970s, the concept of an Asia–Pacific community had emerged, but it was only in the following decade that the concept came to have great significance. In 1982, the US government reported that its trade in the Asia–Pacific region for the first time exceeded its Atlantic trade. This was as clear an indication as any of the rising economic importance of the Asian and Pacific countries. Besides Japan, the so-called 'four dragons' (South Korea, Taiwan, Hong Kong, and Singapore) recorded phenomenal growth rates and came to be referred to as 'newly industrialized countries' (NIC) or 'newly industrialized economies' (NIE). Moreover, China, too, grew fast, its annual rate of growth exceeding 10 per cent during 1984–88. In 1980 the Asian countries produced some 13 per cent of the world's industrial output, but ten years later the ratio had increased to nearly 20 per cent. By then they accounted for almost 30 per cent of the world's industrial exports. Japan, South Korea, and Taiwan were investing huge amounts of money abroad, turning them into some of the prominent creditor nations.

Only a few decades earlier, it had been customary to characterize Asia as a land of over-population and poverty, but the developments in the 1980s were making such notions obsolete. At least in Japan, the NIE, and some of the ASEAN members, population growth had been checked and national incomes increased to such an extent that, if the trend continued, it was expected that by the end of the twentieth century the standard of living of these countries would exceed the levels enjoyed by some European nations. Of course, unlike Europe, the Asia–Pacific region lacked shared religious and historical experiences, and they had divergent political systems, making it more problematical than for European countries to develop an integrated regional community. Still, it would be difficult to deny that some sense of regional identity was already emerging. Japan, for instance, the only participant in the annual 'economic summit', was being urged by other Asian countries to represent their interests in such gatherings. Several Asian leaders were speaking of the need to strengthen intra-regional ties so as not to fall behind other communities.

At the same time, even if regional communities were to develop here and in Europe and North America, it was not considered likely that these communities would fragment the globe, dividing up the world into mutually exclusive units. That was the situation in the 1930s, but fifty years later, there was a new culture abroad, a culture of cross-national connections and shared human consciousness that militated against fragmentation. Democracy, civil society, religion, environmental protection – all such forces were exerting influence across national boundaries, visibly and invisibly penetrating all countries. The spectacular innovations in communications and information technology, ranging from satellite television to fax transmission, from electronic mail to global computer networks, further breached existing sovereign entities. Of course, the new technology could be put to conventional use, in military strategy and economic competition. At the same time, however, there were so many non-strategic uses of the new technology among the mass of people everywhere that it was virtually impossible for any state authority, however authoritarian, to keep the national boundaries closed. The world was already becoming interconnected through electronic networks even before governments were willing to reformulate their policies accordingly.

How far did Japan's leaders and people recognize these revolutionary changes sweeping through the globe, and how did they define their role in such a world? Were some new concepts of Japanese diplomacy emerging? It is not clear if this last question can be answered in the affirmative.

For instance, there was little significant change in Japan's security policy in the 1980s. For one thing, during the first half of the decade, the Japanese government, headed first by Suzuki Zenkō and then by Nakasone Yasuhiro, shared the Reagan administration's perception of the Soviet threat and sought to strengthen the security ties across the Pacific. Suzuki, visiting Washington in 1981, formally used the term 'alliance' in describing Japan–US relations, and, two years later, Nakasone spoke of the two nations' constituting 'a community of destiny'. Such expressions went beyond Japan's passive reliance on the United States for its protection and showed a willingness to cooperate more actively with US military strategy. In 1981 a study group 'to discuss emergencies' was organized. Its aim was to consider joint Japan–US strategy in case of an emergency. The study, completed by 1984, detailed planning about the disposition of forces in a joint strategy in the area. It was particularly notable that in the new plan Japan was assigned the task of patrolling the 1,000-mile 'sea-lanes'. That would cover the wide area from Japan to the central Pacific and the Philippines. In a way, the Japanese navy was going to play a role in the defence of this wide area, hitherto the responsibility of the US navy. After 1980 the two navies joined forces from Australia, New Zealand, and Canada in annual Pacific exercises, the so-called 'Rim-Pac' operations.

Clearly, Japan's role was no longer just passive. It appeared ready to share the burden of self-defence with the United States. The concept of 'burden-sharing', of course, had economic connotations. Many in the United States began asserting that Japan, fast becoming an economic superpower, should do more to help ease the American burden, especially through contributing more to the cost of maintaining US forces there. Such a view sometimes created the criticism that Japan was having 'a free ride' on its defence, especially so since the European allies were earmarking larger portions of their GNPs for defence. To respond to such criticism, Japan took steps to increase its military budget. Between 1980 and 1988, for instance, Japan's GNP increased by less than 50 per cent, but its defence spending grew by more than 60 per cent, corresponding to 0.90 per cent of GNP in 1980 and 1.013 per cent in 1988. As a portion of government outlays, defence spending increased from 5.24 per cent to 6.53 per cent. These were still smaller figures than those of most other countries, not to mention the United States and the Soviet Union, but since the economy kept expanding, even such percentages meant that Japan's military budget was now among the largest in the world. In 1980 it ranked eighth in defence spending behind the United States, the Soviet Union, China, Saudi Arabia, Britain, France, and West Germany, but by 1987 it ranked sixth, and in 1990 third. Whether this was turning Japan into a military superpower was questionable, however. Its security policy still adhered to a 'concentration on defence', and the nation undertook neither nuclear armament nor the development of offensive weapons. Japanese forces were prohibited from being sent abroad. Thus Japan's defence force still had a very restricted existence, a situation that was little different from the Fukuda doctrine of the 1970s that Japan would become an economic but not a military superpower.

There were two problems with such traditionalism, however. First, it suggested that Japanese officials were little interested in developing a new formula for security policy even when the international environment was rapidly changing. Security policy, after all, must be formulated in response to changing military, strategic balances in the world. These changes were clearly taking place, but to maintain the policy that had existed since the 1950s meant that as far as Japan was concerned they did not create a wholly new geopolitical condition. Tokyo's officials apparently reasoned that, with the Soviet Union still a major power in Asia and the Pacific, and with uncertain situations in the Korean peninsula or in Indochina, it was premature to redefine security policy. The end of the Cold War in Europe, in other words, did not seem to mean automatically that in Asia, too, tensions were easing. It was still important to preserve the security ties with the United States and to persist in the long-standing defensive strategy. Whether there was a gap between such thinking and the reality of international relations, and whether Japan should be doing more to prepare for the coming of a post-Cold War era in Asia, were questions few were asking in the 1980s.

Second, the gap between the military and economic aspects of Japan's foreign relations continued to widen. Given the traditional approach to security policy in the face of rapid economic growth, the gap, which had always existed, gave rise to serious questioning abroad. America's criticism of Japan for getting a 'free ride' on defence was one manifestation. Another was the suspicion on the part of Japan's Asian neighbours that it would some day surely seek to utilize its superior economic power for military purposes, a sentiment that came to be heard even in the United States. Such suspicion was fuelled by Japan's tendency to desist from developing a clear definition of foreign policy, instead tending to cope with each diplomatic or security question as it arose. The gap between economic and military power would remain so long as there was no ideology, no intellectual framework, in which to account for the gap, or to narrow it. Neither step was being taken in the 1980s, at least not to the extent of generating a new national consensus. All this created the impression that the Japanese were only interested in their own economic interests and well-being, trying to capture as large a market share abroad as possible, without giving anything in return. At the end of the 1980s, foreign observers noted that a widely read book in Japan was entitled, *A Japan That Can Say No*. It was as if Japan, an economic superpower, was saying 'no' to all pressures and demands from abroad that it should do something to contribute to the international community.

For the time being, in any event, Japanese leaders, political and business, were busy coping with tensions abroad which the nation's economic power was creating. Friction with other countries over trade and investment matters constituted a crucial aspect of Japanese foreign affairs throughout the decade of the 1980s.

The Japanese economy, having successfully surmounted the international monetary crises and the oil shocks of the 1970s, resumed its growth in the 1980s. Its net growth rate after inflation almost always surpassed the rates of other advanced countries, exceeding 4 per cent during the second half of the decade. In 1987, indeed, its nominal per capita income ($19,553) passed America's ($18,570). This, to be sure, reflected the steep rise in the rate of exchange between the yen and the dollar, which was brought about in 1985. But the appreciation of the yen did little to alter the nature of Japanese trade, where exports kept increasing and the trade surplus almost reached $100 billion by 1987. At least statistically, Japan became one of the richest countries in the world, with a huge foreign exchange reserve. To reduce the surplus, the government encouraged Japanese firms and individuals to invest their funds abroad and, quite simply, to spend their money by going overseas. In 1980 some 4 million Japanese went abroad as tourists or students, or else on business, but the number doubled by 1988, indicating that one out of every 14 Japanese was spending some time in a foreign country. Many of them bought expensive paintings and real estate abroad, giving rise to the image of 'the affluent Japanese'. In 1987 the Japanese had amassed overseas assets totalling some $132.8 billion, or about 6 per cent of the GNP. Japan, which till recently had been borrowing money and running trade deficits, was now accumulating huge trade surpluses and lending the money earned by investing it abroad. In the same year Japan's total direct investment overseas amounted to $19.5 billion. A country with a population that was 2.5 per cent of the world's total accounted for 11.2 per cent of its income and 9.8 per cent of its trade. A country that used to assume the posture of a 'have not' nation now came to be seen as a major 'have' nation. Of course, Japan was far from a 'have' nation in terms of natural resources and foodstuffs, for which it was more than ever dependent on foreign supply. But the fact remained that a significant portion of the world's income and funds was concentrated there; Japan's per capita income was 50 times that of China, 10 times that of Turkey, and 8 times that of Brazil.

Was such a situation desirable for the international economy? Was Japan's wealth creating a serious economic disequilibrium in the world? These were questions that began to be raised more and more intensively, and the Japanese government was aware that they must be responded to. The Foreign Ministry's *Blue Book* for 1989, for instance, admitted that 'the biggest challenge for our foreign policy is to make an appropriate contribution to correcting the global disequilibrium'. Specifically, the report listed 'an economic policy stressing domestic consumption, an improvement in market access, and deregulation' as desirable goals. Japan must reformulate its economic policies so as to counter the charge that its surpluses were 'making it difficult to maintain the international economic order'. All these steps would take time, however, and in the meantime serious friction arose with other countries, especially the United States. Its 'Japan bashing', an interesting phenomenon of the 1980s, reflected a sense of frustration with the chronic trade and balance-of-payments deficits the nation had towards Japan, but more fundamentally, it underlined the criticism that Japan, a beneficiary of the postwar international economic system, should be doing more to sustain it. American criticism was not only aimed at these statistics but became very specific, for instance demanding that Japan should do something about its tax policies that favoured banks and export-oriented industry, its generally low interest rates, its exorbitant real estate prices, its protection of farmers, small business enterprises, and local retail stores, and its peculiar business practices such as *keiretsu*. All these policies and practices were cited as examples of Japan's 'closed' society and economy, contrary to the spirit of openness that had underlain the international economic order.

Although not all such criticism was deserved, the Japanese government as well as business and mass media came to take it far more seriously than earlier and took steps to redefine foreign and domestic economic policies. For instance, in order to reduce exports and increase imports, the government pledged that cumbersome regulations would be removed or modified, the distribution and marketing systems would be streamlined, public works (sewer systems, highways, parks) would be expanded, and banking, insurance, and other service industries would be opened to foreign competition. But there was as yet no wholesale design for transforming Japanese society or internationalizing the domestic market. Instead, Japan gave the impression that it was grudgingly taking these measures under foreign pressure (*gaiatsu*). That is why foreign criticism of Japanese economic policies and practices did not abate, which in turn exasperated Japanese officials and public opinion. The popularity of a book like *A Japan That Can Say No* reflected this psychological crisis.

Fortunately, these psychological, emotional tensions did not prevent serious discussion in Japan about the fundamental direction and orientation of its foreign policy. Best exemplified by the popularity of the term 'internationalization', more and more Japanese began insisting that the nation should undertake a serious effort to preserve the system of multilateral trade and investment, thereby demonstrating Japan's commitment to openness and interdependence. The concept of internationalization suggested that Japan should not isolate itself from the world but, on the contrary, that it must integrate itself fully into it. Of course, Japan since 1945 had been 'internationalized' in a general sense, in sharp contrast to the self-chosen path of pan-Asian exclusiveness of the 1930s. Still, internationalization of a defeated nation was rather different from that being demanded of a prosperous member of the world community. It implied that the nation should not simply benefit from, but contribute something to the maintenance of, an open and interdependent international economic order. In practice, this meant playing an active role in bringing the Uruguay Round of trade negotiations (begun in 1986) to a successful conclusion, thereby strengthening GATT, in helping to solve the grave debt problem of the developing countries, and in promoting economic interchanges with the Soviet Union and other East European countries in the wake of the end of the Cold War. But by far the most serious project was to internationalize Japan domestically. American and Japanese officials undertook 'structural innovations initiatives' so as to open up Japanese society to foreign goods, services, capital, and even workers, thereby creating conditions in Japan analogous to those abroad from which Japanese businessmen, goods, and capital had benefited.

Ultimately, these led to the problem of culture, for openness, interdependence, internationalization, and similar concepts related to patterns of thought and behaviour of people. The Japanese economy could never be fully internationalized until the Japanese people had become internationalized, psychologically and intellectually. Liberalization of financial transactions or removal of non-tariff barriers might be accomplished more easily than changes in the people. But until they became less exclusionist, nationalistic, or exceptionalist, thinking that they were a people endowed with a unique culture, the nation would continue to be isolated in the international community. In such a situation, it would be very difficult for the Japanese people 'to make a contribution to the world', as Prime Minister Takeshita Noboru vowed on numerous occasions.

One encouraging sign in this respect was the political leaders' stress on cultural themes, something that had begun earlier but was now promoted with a sense of urgency, as if to define a role for Japan in a changing world. Takeshita, for instance, stated in London in May 1988 that alongside national security and economic growth, 'cultural exchange' now constituted 'the third pillar' of Japanese foreign policy. Not just in promoting the study of Japan abroad, but in many other ways, such as the preservation of historical monuments in, and scholarly exchanges with,

Southeast Asian countries, Japan's cultural diplomacy became more and more active. The Japanese government also showed strong interest in environmental questions, as exemplified by the holding in Tokyo, in September 1989, of a world conference on 'the preservation of earth's environment'. The economic summit held earlier that year in Paris had identified the need to protect rain forests and to prevent desertification in developing countries. Demographic pressures in these lands, too, were threatening rare species of animals and plants. The advanced countries, on their part, were contributing to pollution by vehicle exhaust, and the socialist nations had done massive damage to rivers and forests through their mining and manufacturing programmes with little regard for the environment. These were all enormously complex cultural problems, and if Japan were to be serious about its cultural diplomacy, here was a challenge it could try to meet. Perhaps that was why environmentalism appealed to the Japanese people; it enabled them to define a constructive role in the world that was not military in nature and that went beyond self-enrichment through economic pursuits.

CONCLUSION: JAPAN AND THE WIDER WORLD AT THE END OF THE TWENTIETH CENTURY

In a little more than a century, Japan has gone through spectacular changes in its relationship with the wider world. Starting as a newcomer to the international scene with little to guide its conduct except a determination to emulate the powerful nations of the West, it managed to establish itself as a major Asian power, then the main imperialist in the region, and even a global geopolitical player in but a few decades. Its fall to impotence was just as dramatic, but then, in the second half of the twentieth century, the nation tried a different approach, away from military prowess and imperial domination and more towards concentration on economic pursuits. The international environment tolerated Japan's rise to great-power status during the half-century after the 1880s, till the latter began destroying the structure of world order, an aggression that was met by a world-wide coalition to resist and punish the nation. After Japan's defeat, its economic diplomacy was once again assisted by favourable international circumstances until, once again, the nation's economic power appeared to infringe upon the stability of the world system. At the end of the twentieth century, Japan was being confronted with a new challenge, the challenge of redefining its approach to the external world even as it sought to come face to face with the reality of a rapidly ageing and consumer-oriented society, itself a product of postwar prosperity and peace.

In reviewing the history of Japanese foreign affairs since the late nineteenth century, it is difficult to escape the conclusion that by and large the nation has been a beneficiary of the international environment; its security and economic interests have been ensured by a combination of factors generated elsewhere so that its foreign policy has tended to consist in fitting itself into the environment. That has not required much intellectual effort, and that is why Japanese policy usually gives the impression of passivity or reactivity rather than activity or assertiveness. When the Japanese recognized the need for a greater initiative in defining a less passive role for themselves in the world, the best they could come up with before 1945 was pan-Asianism, postulating a division of the world into East and West. That proved a disastrous path to take; under the self-proclaimed doctrine of Asian coprosperity, the nation engaged in savage acts of aggression and atrocity against Asian and Western peoples. That experience numbed the national psyche after 1945, and for many decades it was difficult even to consider another attempt at reconceptualizing the basis of Japanese foreign affairs.

All this is to suggest that, compared to some of the great powers, Japan has not made sufficiently clear how it proposes to behave in the world, beyond pursuing its own security and economic interests. The nation has not made a notable contribution to the international order. Its foreign affairs have tended to be devoid of a sense of purpose going beyond self-interest. In the meantime, the world has changed and is changing rapidly. Asia, over which it once sought to establish control in the name of awakening its people from passivity, is a dynamic centre of economic activities, something that cannot be said to owe itself to Japanese initiatives. The Cold War, which was a convenient framework into which to fit national security needs, has ended, and various possibilities exist for new groupings of nations. Once again, Japan is being called upon to adapt itself to the external environment. Whether it will be as adept at the task as it was during the Meiji period and after 1945, or whether it will make calamitous choices, as it did in the first decades of the century, remains to be seen. Perhaps neither possibility is likely for the very reason that the rapidly changing world will be less tolerant both of Japanese passivity and of its self-centred activism.

What is Japan to do? It owes the world much. It is time for it to give something in return. At the very least, its people will need to develop a historical perspective so as to understand how the nation has behaved in the world, how it has benefited from the international order, and how it once caused it so much destruction and misery. Japan, in dealing with the external world, must learn to internalize it, to become a contributing member of the international community. The world at the end of the twentieth century holds many possibilities, some more ominous for the future of humanity than others. The Japanese should identify with those people and those forces everywhere that promote greater openness, interdependence, and communication across national boundaries. Such an objective calls for changes within Japan. And indeed the transformation of the nation, and of all nations, and of the world is more than ever interlinked. This is no time to indulge in self-congratulatory parochialisms, holding up the virtues of a nation's history and culture over others. Japan has been particularly guilty of this. It must show that it, too, can change, that it is willing to learn from the past and to join others in contributing to the preservation and consolidation of the world community.

GUIDE TO FURTHER READING

I list below important publications in English that will help the reader obtain additional information and perspectives on the history of modern Japanese foreign affairs.

For the 'opening' of Japan in the mid-nineteenth century and the Meiji government's early foreign relations, probably the best introduction is Marius Jansen, *Japan and Its World* (new edition, Princeton, 1995). An excellent study of Meiji Japan's efforts at developing export trade is provided by Christopher Howe, *The Origins of Modern Japanese Trade Supremacy* (London, 1995). There is surprisingly little in English that describes the revision of 'unequal treaties', but Howe's book presents a detailed discussion of why the abolition of extraterritoriality and the retrocession of tariff autonomy were of critical importance if Japan were to promote overseas trade. Some of these concerns are described on a personal level through the experiences of a Japanese silk merchant in the United States, in Haru Reischauer, *Samurai and Silk* (Cambridge, Mass., 1986). The reader may gain additional insights into the position of Japan in world politics in the 1870s to the 1890s by comparing it with Germany, both 'late-comers' on the international scene. See Bernd Martin, *Germany and Japan in the Modern World* (Providence, Rhode Island, 1995).

For Meiji Japan's early dealings with its Asian neighbours, the best account is Key-Hiuk Kim, *The Last Phase of the East Asian World Order* (Berkeley, 1980). The author chronicles the processes through which the traditional 'Confucian' order in East Asia crumbled under Japan's expansionist thrust. On that thrust, culminating in the war against China

(1894–95) and the emergence of Japan as an imperialist power, we are fortunate to have two superb monographs: Hilary Conroy, *The Japanese Seizure of Korea* (Philadelphia, 1960), and Peter Duus, *The Abacus and the Sword* (Berkeley, 1995). Conroy traces the domestic political currents that produced a movement to expand Japanese influence in Korea from the 1870s to the 1890s, and Duus pays close attention to the actual working of Japanese imperialism on the peninsula. This book is a valuable example of a 'peripheral' approach in which the interactions between Japanese and Koreans are carefully examined. On the military aspect of the Chinese–Japanese war, see Stewart Lone, *Japan's First Modern War* (London, 1994). The best source for official Japanese thinking is the famous memoir written by Foreign Minister Mutsu Munemitsu right after the war, *Kenkenroku*, which has been published in a superb translation by Gordon Berger (Princeton, 1982).

The most reliable study of Japanese imperialism, from the 1890s to its collapse in 1945, is William Beasley, *Japanese Imperialism* (Oxford, 1987). The author's balanced presentation of data makes the book the best introduction to the subject. A major historiographic achievement in the last decades has been the publication of two important collections of scholarly essays: Ramon Myers and Mark Peattie, eds, *The Japanese Colonial Empire* (Princeton, 1984), and Peter Duus, Ramon Myers, and Mark Peattie, eds, *The Japanese Informal Empire in China* (Princeton, 1989). The first contains monographs on Japan's 'formal' empire, including Taiwan and Korea, whereas the second treats the military, political, economic, and cultural control Japan sought to establish over China 'informally', that is, without a formal colonial regime. The line between formal and informal empires is rather tenuous, but, regardless of one's views on such a distinction, the contributors to these volumes, as well as their editors, have added tremendously to our knowledge of modern Japanese imperialism.

Specific examples of Meiji Japan's 'great power' diplomacy may be read in such standard accounts as Ian Nish, *The Anglo-Japanese Alliance* (second edition, London, 1985); John A. White, *The Diplomacy of the Russo-Japanese War* (Princeton, 1964); and Shumpei Okamoto, *The Japanese Oligarchy and the Russo-Japanese War* (New York, 1970).

Michael Blaker, *Japanese International Negotiating Style* (New York, 1977) offers an interesting study of the 'style' of Japanese diplomatic (and, by implication, trade and other) negotiations. The heightening tensions in Japanese relations with the United States around the time of the Russo-Japanese war are put in the framework of the simultaneous emergence of the two nations as imperialists in Akira Iriye, *Pacific Estrangement* (Cambridge, Mass., 1972).

Imperialism, formal or informal, however, is not necessarily the only framework in which we can study Japanese foreign affairs at that time, and I have suggested several other themes in *China and Japan in the Global Context* (Cambridge, Mass., 1992) and in *Cultural Internationalism and World Order* (Baltimore, 1997). On Japan's relations with China in the early twentieth century, the most interesting account is still Marius B. Jansen, *The Japanese and Sun Yat-sen* (Cambridge, Mass., 1954). Jansen has also translated, with Etō Shinkichi, a famous memoir by a Japanese 'shishi' (an unofficial intriguer on the Asian continent), Miyazaki Tōten, *My Thirty-three Years' Dream* (Princeton, 1982). See also several essays included in Akira Iriye, ed., *The Chinese and the Japanese* (Princeton, 1980).

Japan's continental expansion reached a high point during the First World War, the period which not only saw the decline of European influence in Asia but also political instability in China following the overthrow of the Manchu dynasty as well as the collapse of the Romanov dynasty in Russia. Unfortunately, few studies of Japanese foreign affairs of this period have been published in English. But the reader may turn to two superb monographs as a beginning: James William Morley, *The Japanese Thrust into Siberia* (New York, 1957); and Frederick Dickinson, *World War I and Japan* (Cambridge, Mass., 1997). Morley makes use of sources in both Japanese and Russian to examine in detail Japan's Siberian expedition of 1918, while Dickinson examines how Japan's civilian and military leaders shared certain objectives about continental expansion.

The years following the First World War have been studied from various angles. The end of the Anglo-Japanese alliance, which came as a result of the Washington conference of 1921–22, is ably chronicled by Ian Nish, *The Alliance in Decline* (London, 1972). The best study of the

Washington Conference on the basis of Japanese sources is Roger Dingman, *Power in the Pacific* (Chicago, 1976). Focusing on the conference's deliberations on naval disarmament, the author describes how the political leadership in Japan, the United States, and Britain resolved to put an end to a dangerous arms race. For Japanese diplomacy for the rest of the decade, see Akira Iriye, *After Imperialism* (Cambridge, Mass., 1965), a study of how Japan and other nations fared under, and undermined, the 'Washington conference system' of Asian international affairs. Shidehara Kijūrō, the principal exponent of this 'system,' is discussed in Nobuya Bamba, *Japanese Diplomacy in a Dilemma* (Kyoto, 1972). For Tanaka Giichi, often viewed as Shidehara's nemesis, see William Morton, *Tanaka Giichi and Japan's China Policy* (New York, 1980).

If Japan reduced its armaments and desisted from blatant expansionism in the 1920s, it redoubled its efforts to increase its trade and promote close, non-military ties with other countries, especially with China. Concerning its struggle for greater trade competitiveness, see Howe's book cited above. I discussed Japan's 'peaceful expansionism' in the decade in an essay included in Bernard Silberman and Harry Harootunian, eds, *Japan in Crisis* (Princeton, 1974). No scholar has contributed more to the study of Japanese–Chinese cultural relations than Joshua Fogel, whose four books are all based on Japanese and Chinese sources and chronicle a rich story of cultural encounters – by academics, novelists, travellers, and many others – between the two countries: *Politics and Sinology* (Cambridge, Mass., 1984), *Nakae Ushikichi in China* (Cambridge, Mass., 1989), *Literature and Travel in the Japanese Rediscovery of China* (Stanford, 1996), and *The Cultural Dimension of Sino-Japanese Relations* (New York, 1997). Some of these works are less studies of Japanese foreign relations than of 'the sociology of knowledge': how a Japanese comes to have an understanding of China, and what that understanding entails. But these questions are never very far from the day-to-day development of Japanese relations with China, and with other countries.

How the promise of Shidehara's cooperative diplomacy in the 1920s, not just towards China but towards other countries as well, gave way to the openly aggressive, unilateralist approach of the 1930s is a topic that awaits extensive study. Several interpretive essays are contained in James W. Morley, ed., *Dilemma of Growth in Prewar Japan* (Princeton, 1971). For the Manchurian crisis of 1931–32, the point of departure for Japan's renewed aggressiveness, Sadako Ogata's *Defiance in Manchuria* (Berkeley, 1964) is still the best account. As the title suggests, the book focuses on the 'defiance' by Japan's military, in Manchuria, Korea, and Tokyo, in acting independently of the civilian authorities. The question of why the civilian authorities gave in so easily is also addressed. Ian Nish, *Japan's Struggle with Internationalism* (London, 1993), examines how Japanese 'internationalists' struggled, without success, to avoid so drastic a step as the withdrawal from the League of Nations, which was certain to isolate the nation even further from the world community. Stephen S. Large's *Emperor Hirohito and Shōwa Japan* (London, 1992) explores the role of the emperor during the crisis and comes to a conflicting conclusion; on one hand, Hirohito was appalled at the way in which the military seemed to be usurping power and alienating other countries, but, at the same time, he was keenly aware of his constitutional position, which he interpreted to mean 'reigning but not governing', so that he was weary of interposing himself in day-to-day decisions. Another good book is Miles Fletcher, *The Search for a New Order* (Chapel Hill, 1982), a study of several leading intellectuals who embraced various versions of fascism as the system most appropriate to Japan, especially when the world economic crisis after 1929 was creating grave social problems.

The best introduction to the thought and behaviour of the Japanese military during the 1930s is Masao Maruyama, *Thought and Behavior in Modern Japanese Politics* (New York, 1966). See also Richard Storry, *Double Patriots* (Boston, 1957); Mark Peattie, *Ishiwara Kanji and Japan's Confrontation with the West* (Princeton, 1975); and Ben-Ami Shillony, *Revolt in Japan* (Princeton, 1973). The military's stress on self-sufficiency, so as to lessen the nation's dependence on Western resources and goods, is ably examined by James B. Crowley, *Japan's Quest for Autonomy* (Princeton, 1966), and Michael Barnhart, *Japan Prepares for Total War* (Ithaca, 1987).

Japanese foreign affairs during the 1930s, starting with

the conquest of Manchuria and culminating in the final crisis and war with the United States and Great Britain in 1941, are surveyed by Akira Iriye, *The Origins of the Second World War in Asia and the Pacific* (London, 1987). For more details, the reader should turn to the five volumes that have been published under the overall title of *The Road to the Pacific War*. These volumes contain articles originally published in Japan during 1962–63. Although more than thirty years have passed since their publication, they remain fresh and insightful, an invaluable point of departure for any systematic study of Japan's road to war. The English translation has been undertaken by a team organized and supervised by James W. Morley. The titles of the five volumes are: *Japan Erupts* (New York, 1984); *The China Quagmire* (New York, 1992); *Deterrent Diplomacy* (New York, 1976); *The Fateful Choice* (New York, 1987); and *The Final Confrontation* (New York, 1994).

The study of Japan's road to war has been notable because it has been an instance of remarkable international scholarship. Japanese and non-Japanese historians have organized conferences and published jointly-authored books. As a result, this, the most disastrous period in modern Japanese history, has been the most fruitful in terms of promoting international scholarly cooperation. Space allows only a short listing of some examples of collaborative work. Akira Iriye and Warren Cohen, eds, *American, Chinese, and Japanese Perspectives on Wartime Asia* (Wilmington, Del., 1984) is a collection of essays written by historians from the three countries who met together over a period of time to exchange ideas. Dorothy Borg and Shumpei Okamoto, eds, *Pearl Harbor as History* (New York, 1973) is a product of Japanese and American researchers who brought their papers together for intensive discussion in 1969. Likewise, Ian Nish, ed., *Anglo-Japanese Alienation* (London, 1980) contains essays originally presented at a binational conference in 1979.

Many excellent studies exist on the Japanese–US crisis of 1941 that resulted in war. See, in particular, Robert Butow, *John Doe Associates* (Stanford, 1974), an analysis of last-minute negotiations in Washington to avert a final break; Waldo H. Heinrichs, *Threshold of War* (New York, 1988), a close examination of President Franklin D.

Roosevelt's strategy in the crucial months following Germany's invasion of the Soviet Union in June 1941; Jonathan Marshall, *To Have and Have Not* (Berkeley, 1995), a study of how US officials became convinced that the nation had to defend Southeast Asian resources against Japanese expansion; and John Stephan, *Hawaii under the Rising Sun* (Honolulu, 1990), a fascinating account of how segments of the Japanese population in Hawaii supported the war in China and welcomed the war against the United States.

For Japanese relations with Britain on the eve of the Second World War, see Peter Lowe, *Great Britain and the Origins of the Pacific War* (Oxford, 1977). For Germany, both John Fox, *Germany and the Far Eastern Crisis* (Oxford, 1982) and the above-noted book by Martin are useful. Fox explains why Adolf Hitler decided to support Japan against China in 1937–38, and Martin compares Japanese with German totalitarianism. For the long war between Japan and China during 1937–45, John H. Boyle, *China and Japan at War* (Stanford, 1972) is still useful, although we need a fresh study on the basis of Chinese archives, both on the mainland and in Taiwan, which have begun to be opened up. In the meantime, Youli Sun, *China and the Origins of the Pacific War* (New York, 1993) and Parks Coble, *Facing Japan* (Cambridge, Mass., 1991) both contain useful data on Chinese politicians, intellectuals, and others as they faced the Japanese threat during the 1930s.

There is an enormous amount of literature on Japan during the Second World War. The two best surveys are Ben-Ami Shillony, *Politics and Culture in Wartime Japan* (New York, 1981) and Thomas Havens, *The Valley of Darkness* (New York, 1978). For an account written by a Japanese historian, see Saburō Ienaga, *The Pacific War* (New York, 1976). Theodore and Haruko Cook's *Japan at War* (New York, 1992) is an excellent compilation of reminiscences by Japanese (in the 1970s and the 1980s) about the war. See also Mark and Kyoko Selden, *The Atomic Bomb* (New York, 1989), similarly a collection of voices from Japan about the atomic bombing. On Japanese policy and strategy in the war against the United States, see my *Power and Culture* (Cambridge, Mass., 1981) in which I argue that, despite their deadly struggle in the Pacific, Japanese officials eventually came to accept a view of Asian international relations that approximated the American visions as expressed, for instance, in the Atlantic charter. John Dower, *War without Mercy* (New York, 1986), as well as chapters from the same author's *Japan in War and Peace* (New York, 1993), describe in detail Japanese and American views of one another during the war; not surprisingly, they were extremely negative, making the two countries' postwar reconciliation all the more remarkable.

Historians have been increasingly turning their attention to what went on in those parts of Asia that were occupied by Japanese forces. The most up-to-date scholarship on this subject is represented in the essays collected in Peter Duus, Ramon Myers, and Mark Peattie, eds, *The Japanese Wartime Empire* (Princeton, 1996). The contributors look at Taiwan, Korea, Northeast and North China, and Southeast Asian countries and examine the political, economic, social, and cultural consequences of Japanese rule. Also useful are Theodore Friend, *The Blue-Eyed Enemy* (Princeton, 1988), focusing on the Philippines and Indonesia, and Grant Goodman, ed., *Japanese Cultural Politics in Southeast Asia during World War 2* (New York, 1991), describing various wartime programmes, such as student exchanges, designed to bring Japanese and the people of occupied areas closer together.

On the steps leading to Japan's decision to surrender, Robert Butow, *Japan's Decision to Surrender* (Stanford, 1955) is still useful, as are Martin Sherwin, *A World Destroyed* (New York, 1973) and Large's study of the emperor mentioned above. The question of whether the dropping of atomic bombs was really necessary to bring about the surrender has been debated endlessly, among the most recent works being Leon Sigal, *Fighting to a Finish* (Ithaca, 1988), and Gar Alperovitz, *The Decision to Use the Atomic Bomb* (rev. edn, New York, 1995).

There are few systematic surveys of post-1945 Japanese foreign affairs, fundamentally because the bulk of archival material in Japan remains closed. There are, however, some important exceptions. To begin with, much valuable work has been published about the US occupation of Japan, although most of it written in English deals with the United States' policies and objectives in the defeated nation. But some have examined the Japanese side of the picture and argued, on the whole persuasively, that Japanese leaders and officials were no mere receptacles of US-imposed reforms but sought, often successfully, to make their imput. A striking example may be seen in Kyoko Inoue, *MacArthur's Japanese Constitution* (Chicago, 1991), which shows how Japanese politicians, bureaucrats, and scholars managed to translate the English text of the draft constitution in such a way as to preserve as many traditional values and practices as possible. That there was a great deal of continuity between prewar and postwar Japan has been argued most powerfully by John Dower, whose essays in the above-mentioned *Japan in War and Peace*, as well as his *Empire and Aftermath* (Cambridge, Mass., 1979) are required reading for those interested in following certain key individuals and groups who remained virtually unchanged after the war.

On the other hand, there is little doubt that postwar Japanese foreign policy, in contrast to the earlier epoch, was much more devoted to the pursuit of economic than to military objectives, entrusting national security to the protection offered by the US alliance. The genesis of this policy, as well as Japan's limited armament in the 1950s and beyond, are well described in John Welfield, *An Empire in Eclipse* (London, 1988). Security, economic, and other aspects of Japanese relations with the United States during the 1950s and the 1960s are examined by the contributors to Akira Iriye and Warren Cohen, eds, *The United States and Japan in the Postwar World* (Lexington, Ken., 1989). For the political tensions the security alliance with the United States produced, see George Packard, *Protest in Tokyo* (Princeton, 1966), a study of the 1960 riots in Japan against the government's attempt to force through the Diet a new security treaty with the United States. Edwin O. Reischauer, who became US ambassador to Japan in the wake of the turmoil, has published a useful memoir, *My Life between Japan and America* (New York, 1986).

There are several reliable accounts of Japanese foreign affairs since the 1970s. Two recent books focus on Japan's defence industry and examine the issue of domestic weapons production versus reliance on US arms: Michael J. Green, *Arming Japan* (New York, 1995), and Neil Renwick, *Japan's Alliance Politics and Defence Production* (London,

1995). Regarding the often acrimonious trade dispute that developed between the two countries, the best place to begin may be I. M. Destler, Haruhiro Fukui, and H. Sato, *The Textile Wrangle* (Ithaca, 1979), a detailed study of the textile issue that arose in the 1960s. Valuable insights into Japan's economic diplomacy, focusing on the role of the Ministry of International Trade and Industry, are provided by Chalmers Johnson, *MITI and the Japanese Miracle* (Stanford, 1982), and Daniel Okimoto, *Between MITI and the Market* (Stanford, 1989). Many books have chronicled Japan's rise to the status of economic superpower and the implications of this for its relationship with the United States and other countries. Among the most interesting are Paul Kennedy, *The Rise and Fall of the Great Powers* (New York, 1987), and Joseph Nye, *Bound to Lead* (Boston, 1990). Ezra Vogel, *The Four Little Dragons* (Cambridge, Mass., 1992) discusses the degree to which Japan's prewar and postwar economic successes may be said to have contributed to the Asian economic miracle of the 1970s and beyond.

On Japan's postwar relations with the Soviet Union (now Russia), the best survey is Joachim Glaubitz, *Between Tokyo and Moscow* (London, 1995), which is solidly based on Russian and Japanese material. Nothing comparable exists on Japanese–Chinese relations, but Allen S. Whiting, *China Eyes Japan* (Berkeley, 1989) offers an interesting survey of Chinese attitudes towards Japan, including the question of Japan's war guilt. On this last issue, one of the most penetrating accounts is Ian Buruma, *The Wages of Guilt* (New York, 1992), in which the author carefully compares German and Japanese views of the last war.

Numerous essays have been published on Japan's emerging role in the post-Cold War world, in particular in the Asia–Pacific region. Very few of them are of more than journalistic interest: for instance, Gerald L. Curtis, *The United States, Japan, and Asia* (New York, 1994); and Michael Armacost, *Friends or Rivals?* (New York, 1996). This last, by a former US ambassador to Japan, provides an in-depth look at the implications of the end of the Cold War for Japanese–US relations, but in many ways 'friends or rivals?' would seem to sum up the key question the Japanese and other nations have been asking themselves.

INDEX

INDEX

211